Darlene,

Thank you so much
for your encouragement
and your love. You
have such a bright light
so continue to shine!

Love Always,

Genesis 50:20

#JWGIRL4LIFE
Where the Light Meets the Dark

The Journal of Julie Keene
A 90 Day Devotional

Just Susan Publishing
Poplarville, MS 39470

Just Susan Publishing
45 Buford Lane
Poplarville, MS 39470
www.jacobswellrecoverycenter.com

This book is a biography of Susan Haynes Brogan.

Copyright © 2016 by Julie Keene

First Paperback edition February 2016

Designs by Matt Thone
Photographs by Cindy Gustafson

Manufactured in the United States of America

Scriptures referred to in this book are taken from the most up to date translation of the of the Holy Bible published by Zondervan Publishing House and provided online by biblegateway.com

ISBN-13: 978-0692640760 (Just Susan Publishing)

ISBN-10: 0692640762

Dedication Page

This book is dedicated to the women of Jacob's Well Recovery Center – Past, Present, and Future. Here is a call to action for anyone who dares take part in such a radical move of God.

All I can do sometimes to hold it together is just that - hold it together. My flesh is eating away at me and I tremble from my little dose of reality. My heart is broken, but I am allowing God to stitch it up. He is flooding me with His peace, even though each stitch feels like a hot knife. The soothing balm of the blood of Jesus is immediately applied as God mends my heart.

Psalm 147:3 (NIV) - He heals the broken hearted and binds up their wounds.

I told someone yesterday that being on the battlefield is tough. I get knocked down and slapped around by the enemy on a consistent basis. I fall flat on my back on the cold, wet ground and all I can do is look up into the sky as a war rages around me. As soon as I stagger again to my feet, brush myself off, thank God for His protective armor, and pull my sword from my sheath, I'm down again. Here is the thing. There is nowhere on else on the planet I would rather be. I am a soldier in the army that is rising out of Jacob's Well Ministries. I am proud to call that place my home. I am blessed to walk exhausted and blind through the smoke on the battlefield of what each day brings. I am grateful for the gifted and anointed people who fight beside me. The Holy Spirit resides there, the angelic army of the Living God is encamped there, and hope reigns in the hearts of the women who are fresh off their own battlefield, who have gone there for mending. Nothing beats stepping over the threshold from a day of work to smell a home cooked meal wafting in waves of welcome from the kitchen. Everyone claps and cheers in greeting as each person walks through the door. It is a family. Therein lies hope for a generation that should have been lost. There is a legacy being left. Worship is impulsive and uninterrupted. Joy and laughter ring from every corner of the house. The hits keep coming at me, but all they do as serve as a reminder of the promises God gave me. If Satan comes against me so severely, what does he know about my Kingdom purpose that I don't know that he pummels me this hard?

Deuteronomy 20:1-4 (NIV) - When you go to war against your enemies and see horses and chariots and an army greater than yours, do not be afraid of them, because the Lord your God, who brought you up out of Egypt, will be with you. 2 When you are about to go into battle, the priest shall come forward and address the army. 3 He shall say: "Hear, Israel: Today you are going into battle against your enemies. Do not be fainthearted or afraid; do not panic or be terrified by them. 4 For the Lord your God is the one who goes with you to fight for you against your enemies to give you victory."

I came to Jacob's Well broken seemingly beyond repair. I had been living on the streets addicted to anything and everything. Addiction breeds selfishness. I was lost to my own thinking which always landed me on another corner in another city. Even when clean, it was all about me and everyone else was to blame. After coming to Jacob's Well Recovery Center for Women, a Christ centered addiction recovery center, a healing place, a safe haven for greatness, God moved in my life and I had a choice to make. I could either stay stuck in the darkness of my depraved mind, or I could expose it to the Light of Truth and Salvation. Learning the truth about who Julie Keene is was uncomfortable at best, but the relief that came in the process was amazingly bearable. I was afforded not just one, but two 6 month stays at this anointed work and worship program. I came back the second time because my unwillingness to expose the WHOLE truth the first time became evident in my walk in the world. It became my sanctuary.

Ruth 1:16 - *Where you go I will go, and where you stay I will stay. Your people will be my people and your God my God.*

I see women transformed by the Love of Christ on a daily basis. I, myself, am still being changed by His grace. God is Love and Jacob's Well is a perfect example of the love Jesus had for the people. Jesus walked with, talked to, and ministered to tax collectors, prostitutes, lepers, the poor, the fatherless, widows, and the throw-aways of society. He loved the down trodden and He came to save the lost and to give hope to them <u>if they were willing to be transformed.</u>

Psalm 51:12-13 - *Restore to me the joy of your salvation and grant me a willing spirit, to sustain me. 13 Then I will teach transgressors your ways, so that sinners will turn back to you*.

Susan Haynes Brogan says it best, "Jesus has two powers, the power to save and the power to transform. Everyone desires to be saved, but are you willing to undergo the hard process of transformation?" Transformation for me was the toughest part, but I thank God for the people of Jacob's Well showing me the purpose behind the pain. I had to let go of a LOT, but he hardest thing I learned to let go of was MYSELF and my own selfish desires.

Romans 12:2 - Do not conform to the pattern of this world, but be transformed by the renewing of your mind. Then you will be able to test and approve what God's will is—his good, pleasing and perfect will.

Today, I am making a heartfelt plea. Jacob's Well is being pushed by God onto a battlefield never before trekked. They are on a pioneering adventure and their goal is to snatch as many wounded souls from the fire and bring them into the healing hospital God is attempting to build. Jacob's Well currently holds 30 women plus a small staff made up of former graduates. The Haynes family began this ministry and were called to do so out of their own brokenness and redemption. Their hearts desire is to bring Jacob's Well right into the eye of a brewing cataclysmic social storm and open doors for entire families to be brought from the realms of this dying world and into the life sustaining mercy and grace of Christ. The hope is for generations to come.

Exodus 20:5-6 (NIV) - You shall not bow down to them or worship them; for I, the Lord your God, am a jealous God, punishing the children for the sin of the parents to the third and fourth generation of those who hate me, 6 but showing love to a thousand generations of those who love me and keep my commandments.

They are preparing a place of refuge, a home where the face of addiction can be changed, where entire armies of families can be trained for the Kingdom battles that are to come, and where restoration can happen. So many people turn their heads to the addicted society and pay them no mind, but in doing so they are accepting the fact that addiction is killing our nation and the generation behind us is being left behind in foster homes and being written off only to grow up and do the exact same thing. Silence is acceptance. Don't be silent any longer. Your voice will ring loud and clear against this epidemic when you sow a seed today.

I am crying out from the depths of my soul to anyone reading this to be moved by the Spirit of God to donate to the #redefiningrecovery movement. This life given to us by God is not our own. It is to bring others into His loving arms and show them a new way to live. Your donation will SAVE LIVES, restore children to their parents, and all of them will be equally yoked under the blood stained banner of our Savior!
Please visit **www.fundly.com/redefiningrecovery** to learn more about this life sustaining ministry, it's founders, it's graduates, and how you, too, can change the world. God is calling YOU to this Kingdom purpose. Please don't shy away. Also, you can visit us on Facebook at **www.facebook.com/redefiningrecovery** and our website **www.jacobswellrecoverycenter.com** for more information.

Thank you for reading this, thank you for your willingness to be part of the Great Commission, and thank you for allowing hope to rise in the spirits of individuals, children, men, and women that we still have yet to meet. Start a chain that cannot be broken by the enemy! Be the tie that binds!

Isaiah 61
The Spirit of the Sovereign Lord is on me,
because the Lord has anointed me
to proclaim good news to the poor.
He has sent me to bind up the broken hearted,
to proclaim freedom for the captives
and release from darkness for the prisoners,
2 to proclaim the year of the Lord's favor
and the day of vengeance of our God,
to comfort all who mourn,
3 and provide for those who grieve in Zion—
to bestow on them a crown of beauty

instead of ashes,
the oil of joy
instead of mourning,
and a garment of praise
instead of a spirit of despair.
They will be called oaks of righteousness,
a planting of the Lord
for the display of his splendor.
4 They will rebuild the ancient ruins
and restore the places long devastated;
they will renew the ruined cities
that have been devastated for generations.
5 Strangers will shepherd your flocks;
foreigners will work your fields and vineyards.
6 And you will be called priests of the Lord,
you will be named ministers of our God.
You will feed on the wealth of nations,
and in their riches you will boast.
7 Instead of your shame
you will receive a double portion,
and instead of disgrace
you will rejoice in your inheritance.
And so you will inherit a double portion in your
land,
and everlasting joy will be yours.
8 "For I, the Lord, love justice;
I hate robbery and wrongdoing.
In my faithfulness I will reward my people
and make an everlasting covenant with them.
9 Their descendants will be known among the
nations
and their offspring among the peoples.
All who see them will acknowledge
that they are a people the Lord has blessed."
10 I delight greatly in the Lord;
my soul rejoices in my God.
For he has clothed me with garments of salvation
and arrayed me in a robe of his righteousness,

as a bridegroom adorns his head like a priest,
and as a bride adorns herself with her jewels.
11 For as the soil makes the sprout come up
and a garden causes seeds to grow,
so the Sovereign Lord will make righteousness
and praise spring up before all nations.

# Prologue

"Hi, my name is Julie and I am an addict." That is how I used to introduce myself at Anonymous Meetings when I was there seeking a "Higher Power" to save me from myself. I didn't even know what to believe in other than the lies the enemy told me. I idolized all the wrong things and ended up making excuse after excuse in order to continue to check out of my self-inflicted, painful life that was created out of my own victimization, guilt, shame, remorse, and FEAR.

2 Timothy 1:7 - For the Spirit God gave us does not make us timid, but gives us power, love and self-discipline.

I suffered from addiction for over 20 years. After the suicide of my father in 1992, I went on a bender that seemed would never end. Somehow I was able to graduate from high school and college, work, get married, have children, and survive, all while suffering in silence and harming everyone who loved me and cared for me. I was lost, I was broken, my marriage ended, I lost custody of my children, and I tried to end it all. Life as I knew it was a living hell. I was playing roles every moment of every day. I can say I tried, but to me trying means being inactive and complaining about it. I did a lot of that. I moved states, recovery centers, detox centers, anonymous rooms, churches, and another broken marriage....all searching for truth.

I took on two personalities, one that helped me survive in the ghetto when I was trying to score, and one that I had to survive the work force and the demands of being a wife and mother, both for which I was completely unprepared. I was addicted to MORE, to everything, to anything. My addiction took me places I never belonged, designer drugs were traded for hard core street drugs when the high was no longer satisfying my desire to run from myself and the depression that wracked my entire spiritual being, it cost me more than I could pay, and kept me longer than I wanted to stay. I was stuck and saw no way out, so I used that as an excuse to stay checked out of life as well.

Hindsight is 20/20 and looking back I can clearly see the lies that entered my spirit long before I ever took the first drug or ingested the first drink. Excuses are the bricks that build a house of failure and I was full of them. More was never enough. I was putty in the hands of the enemy. My addiction was triggered by my inability to cope with life in general.

I had a desire to feel accepted from a very young age. My dad had gone to prison when I was in the 5th grade and needless to say, my entire life as I knew it was thrown up into the air and landed back on the ground not even resembling the way it was before. It was a nightmare of epic proportions in the mind of an intuitive adolescent girl who thrived in controlled environments. The spirits of rejection and abandonment took over my life and my being. The thing is I realize now that life is all about choices. Was I able to make choices about my future at such a young age? No. Was I able to grasp the reality of what was taking place in the peripherals? Absolutely not. Was I able to truly handle the deceit of the person I trusted the most? No way. However, I was able to make decisions as I grew older, and I feel like "triggers" are just another pretext used to check out of life. I made my own choices. I stepped in my own holes. There is no real justification for why I chose a path of self destruction, other than I just did. To place blame on ANYTHING would be completely unfair. I stood there for the majority of my adult life, blame-thrower in hand, ready to fire. I triggered myself.

I moved from Virginia to Mississippi after a horrible relapse and another stay at another treatment center where I knew all the answers in order to get by and get out, quickly. I did what I always did best and separated my head from my heart and ran. I ran away from responsibility again and justified every single step that I took that would get me further away from the truth of who I was. Geographical cures do not work because the enemy is always waiting at the front door of every new location, unless you are carrying Jesus with you, and I wasn't. I found myself on the street again, living in abandoned houses or sheds, giving myself away, piece by piece, in order to get the next high.

There was a street in Meridian, MS that I called home and every day as I walked my beat I passed an abandoned house on Royal Road that seemed like the perfect location to get away, to use my drug of choice without interruption, to sleep when able. However, every time I passed that house and went to step foot on the property, I was pushed back by some unseen force that wasn't familiar to me. I would like to call it "fear", but it was much deeper than that, the feeling that I got each time I went to defile that old house. I pondered it time and again as I walked, watching it from the other side of the street. I left the streets of Meridian, checked into rehab number 10, and tried again to find hope in a "Higher Power" in anonymous rooms. I left Meridian and traded those streets for the horrific ghetto of Hattiesburg, MS. I died on the street in Hattiesburg after several vain attempts to secure myself a bed at a place called Jacob's Well Recovery Center for Women. I was penniless, hopeless, and completely lost. I had heard about Jacob's Well from a counselor at a treatment center that kicked me out because I had no insurance. I had only been there 2 days when they found out about my dire situation and sent me back out to the streets that consumed me. And then it happened. Jesus found me!!

It was May 25, 2013. Two days after my first dad would have been 51 years old. I was still in bondage and a victim of circumstance and choices. I was alone; my marriage of only 3 short months was coming to an end. I was broke. I was scared. I was living on the street. I hadn't eaten or slept in days. And then it happened, a miracle like no other. I was walking down the street to the house I had been staying at, and I fell out from an accidental overdose. As my body shut down and I stopped breathing I felt more lost than at any other time in my life. Cars were passing by and not even stopping. I was completely aware that my body was shutting down and there wasn't a person around who cared. The next thing I knew, I was walking down the street again. I felt the gravel in my hair and on my clothes and I couldn't even turn around because I was afraid I would see my own body lying there. I was a dead woman walking. I went to the house and sat on the porch and pondered if this was what hell was like. I waited for the sun to go down, which meant that the world was still turning and I was still alive (by no means of my own). And then I fell into a deep sleep.

All throughout the night I was vaguely aware of the chaos that surrounded me. My senses were wide open to the truth of what my life was at that very given moment. I can imagine the angels that were encamped around me for protection. When the sun began to peek over the trees, I heard a still, small voice calling me to walk. And walk I did. A Jesus I still had yet to know picked me up out of my brokenness and the only Being in the universe that has the power to save and the power to transform entered my life. I walked away from that porch, from that street, and found myself the very next day walking across the doorframe of Jacob's Well, by the grace of God. After graduation, I saw a picture on Susan Haynes Brogan's (the President of Jacob's Well) Facebook page that stopped my heart yet again. It was a picture of an old abandoned house, on Royal Road in Meridian, MS. It was the house where the Holy Spirit came through the Haynes family like a flood and their lives were changed. It is the house where their lives ended and a new life with Jesus began. It was the very same house I used to cruise by.

There are no coincidences in this life. Every single step is guided by God and the way is prepared, even in the darkest moments when we see no end to our suffering and our pain. He is always with us. I am now a retired staff member of Jacob's Well, a faithful employee of Jacob's Well Furniture, a lifelong friend and family member to the Haynes, and a trusted servant of God Himself. I am honored to continue to work beside such amazing people who love God more than their own lives. I am blessed to have such an awesome family to come home to from time to time, and I am humbled by the things I get to do for others as I counsel them and minister to them out of my own painful past. God brings everything "full circle".

Jesus' sacrifice for me allows me to wake up every morning and do everything I can to get it right, to continue to press on even when things are tough, to see the potential in every single thing I touch. I was messed up, broken, bruised, ashamed, and fighting for my life from the streets that consumed me. I am being put back together and my broken heart is being mended.

Genesis 50:20 - *You intended to harm me, but God intended it for good to accomplish what is now being done, the saving of many lives.*

Today, I sit in victory over satan because of the sacrifice Jesus made for me on the cross. He died in my place so

I could be set free! The battle is still raging around me, but I am safe in the storm. I came into the world free and intend to leave the same way. The Lord is using my test as a Testimony to His saving grace and I want to give a voice to those suffering in silence. He is bringing it all back around for His glory! I had to come to the realization that I am not perfect, nor will I ever be until I see Him face to face in heaven. I had to loose myself from old ways of thinking and fully surrender everything in my life to Him.

Today, I hold onto promises. I hold onto truth. I hold onto hope. In the eyes of the world, I will always be an addict, I will be labeled as a terrible mother, and I will be rejected by a society that lives in shallow boxes, but God...

God says that I am fearfully and wonderfully made. He says that I am the head and not the tail. He says that He will never leave me, nor forsake me. God says that He will repay me for all the years that I have squandered, the years the locusts have eaten. He says in His awesome Word that I am worthy, I am loved, I am blessed, I am equipped for His service, and I am FREE!

I was in exile. I was lost. I was captive to my own depravity and my own circumstances had me bound to the floor by chains that I put on my own limbs and attached to with locks so tight I couldn't move. Today, I seek God with all my heart and I find Him EVERYWHERE! My future is bright and I do have hope! My desire is to see more people come to know Jesus in an intimate way. I long to see the light come on in eyes that were so veiled that brilliance no longer shone from them. I want to see people free from the bondage that so easily entangles. I have a purpose and it is to be part of the Great Commission. I am ready and I am able!

Galatians 5:1 - It is for freedom that Christ has set us free. Stand firm, then, and do not let yourselves be burdened again by a yoke of slavery.

The following pages depict my walk through recovery in Christ. They are from my own personal journals that I have held onto for dear life because of the great lessons I learned as I stepped out in faith on a daily basis, closer to my Lord and further away from the depravity of my past. Each entry is a direct, front row view into my heart. I went through Jacob's Well Recovery Center the first time as a married woman to another recovering addict. I graduated and lived life as a housewife and then manager of a retail chain. A relapse sent us both careening in opposite directions and divorce was imminent. I returned to Jacob's Well, graduated, and stayed on as staff with my new family. I have a beautiful life today all because of the sacrifices made by the ones who gave their lives so that I could be set free!!

I am honored to be a #JWGIRL4LIFE!
(Jacob's Well Girl for LIFE)

PART ONE

SURRENDER

My First Stay at Jacob's Well Recovery Center for Women

PART ONE
TABLE OF CONTENTS

ONE – *Hindrances*

June 27th – 2013 – Day 32 - I got to talk to my husband this morning. We only got 15 minutes and he was half asleep. I kept trying to figure out things to talk about. I don't even know how to talk to him. I feel like I am trying to control him and over the phone, no less. I need to let him lead and that is so hard. Sometimes I am so over this place and these people. I feel like I am setting myself up for a fall, I can feel it.

But I absolutely must give it to God and continue to do the right thing on purpose. He loves me because HE is GOD, not because I am good (because I'm not good). I need to stop living emotionally and start living on purpose. The definition of the word "hinder" is to cause delay or interruption, to prevent from doing or happening, to stop, to be an obstacle or impediment. Ok...gosh, that fits me on so many levels it's not even funny.

I am a hindrance to myself, to my recovery, to my walk with the Lord. I am a hindrance to my husband from doing what the Lord has purposed him to do. I am a hindrance to the women at Jacob's Well. My opinions are so important these days that it keeps others from wanting to even have one in my presence. NASTY ME!! I am not content with anything. All of this is stemming because I am not getting my way. I am so ungrateful right now and I hate that about myself. I am a barrier to myself, to God, and to people in general. It's time to go to the Word.

Matthew 8:5-6 – When Jesus had entered Capernaum, a centurion came to him, asking for help. "Lord," he said, "my servant lies at home and paralyzed, suffering terribly."

A centurion was a Roman soldier and officer who had control over 100 soldiers. Roman soldiers were hated by the Jews because they were oppressive and controlling (Uh, conviction). Yet, this man came to Jesus and in turn threw aside every obstacle that could stand in the way of getting to him - those being pride, doubt, and power. He did not allow any barriers to block his approach to the One who could save his friend. So why am I putting up barriers to the Lord? Why can't I just be still and content and stop being such a nuisance?

John 6:35,48-51,57-58,60 – Then Jesus declared, "I am the bread of life. Whoever comes to me will never go hungry, and whoever believes in me will never be thirsty." "I am the bread of life. Your ancestors ate the manna in the wilderness, yet they died. But here is the bread that comes down from heaven. Whoever eats this bread will live forever. This bread is my flesh, which I will give for the life of the world." "Just as the living Father sent me and I live because of the Father, so the one who feeds on me will live because of me. This is the bread that came down from heaven. Your ancestors ate manna and died, but whoever feeds on this bread will live forever." On hearing it, many of his disciples said, "This is a hard teaching. Who can accept it?"

I love this! People in the desert with Moses were fed manna every single day, bread from heaven, and they eventually passed away. But Jesus is the bread of life! Eating it will help me see with the eye of faith. It will drive away the enemy. It will give me eternal life and satisfy and sustain my new spiritual life. This will allow me change, to become a help and not a hindrance. That, I cannot do alone.

Philippians 4:11-13 – I am not saying this because I am in need, for I have learned to be content whatever the circumstances. I know what it is to be in need, and I know what it is to have plenty. I have learned the secret of being content in any and every situation, whether well fed or hungry, whether living in plenty or in want. I can do all things through him who gives me strength.

2 – Complaining

June 28th – 2013 – Day 33 - I have one great day, then a bad day, then a great day, then a bad day. Stringing days together without an attack from satan is like trying to climb a ladder without rungs. It seems impossible. I am freaking out about my lack of control over EVERYHING and that has me in such a foul place. This is SO HARD being here. I don't know what to do. So I start complaining, a lot. I do most of it in my thoughts because there is a part of me that doesn't want to hurt anyone's feelings.

Truth be told, I just don't want to get pulled into the counseling room for speaking so negatively out loud. Mandy came today to give us a devotion and I started working on it and looking up ways to combat this unseen enemy. She said some pretty amazing things today that stuck. She said, "When things seem so hard, that means I am growing. I need to recognize my weaknesses." This is my favorite part! She said, "Until I learn how to glorify God by my attitude, I will not be delivered." OK then!! Now what?

Deuteronomy 30:11 – Now what I am commanding you today is not too difficult for you or beyond your reach.

The Lord will give me His Spirit to help me. But unless I can learn to live without, then I can't live with Him.

John 14:16 – And I will ask the Father, and he will give you another advocate to help you and be with you forever.

Things get hard when I am trying to do them ALONE, without God's help. If everything in life were easy, then I would not need the power of the Holy Spirit to help do for me what I cannot do for myself.

Luke 4:1-13 - Jesus, full of the Holy Spirit, left the Jordan and was led by the Spirit into the wilderness, where for forty days he was tempted by the devil. He ate nothing during those days, and at the end of them he was hungry. The devil said to him, "If you are the Son of God, tell this stone to become bread." Jesus answered, "It is written: 'Man shall not live on bread alone.'" The devil led him up to a high place and showed him in an instant all the kingdoms of the world. And he said to him, "I will give you all their authority and splendor; it has been given to me, and I can give it to anyone I want to. If you worship me, it will all be yours." Jesus answered, "It is written: 'Worship the Lord your God and serve him only.'" The devil led him to Jerusalem and had him stand on the highest point of the temple. "If you are the Son of God," he said, "throw yourself down from here. For it is written: "'He will command his angels concerning you to guard you carefully; they will lift you up in their hands, so that you will not strike your foot against a stone.'" Jesus answered, "It is said: 'Do not put the Lord your God to the test.' When the devil had finished all this tempting, he left him until an opportune time.

Jesus didn't complain, he didn't think negatively, and he didn't get confused. Wow. satan is a liar, he tempts me with things that are comfortable - mainly my old behaviors. No wonder it's so hard. I allow it to happen and I don't stand on the Rock of my salvation. I do the evil inside of me that I don't want to do. If I don't give up, don't lose heart, then I will eventually reap the rewards.

Philippians 4:6 – Do not be anxious about anything, but in every situation, by prayer and petition, with thanksgiving, present your requests to God.

Murmuring, grumbling, faultfinding, and complaining usually occur in my life when something has not gone the way I wanted it to or when I have had to wait for something longer than I expected. Patience is not the ability to wait, but the ability to keep a good attitude while waiting. I can overcome complaining by making the most of Christ within me.

3 – *Salvation*

July 2nd – 2013 – Day 37 - I am so tired. I am sick and tired of living for myself and allowing satan to use me. Last night, Brother Ray did a devotion. He quoted:

John 8:36 – If the Son sets you free, you will be free indeed.

He said, "This is the Bible," as he held up the big book in his hand. I rolled my eyes and sat back for a long evening. He continued, "These are Basic Instructions Before Leaving Earth!" For the first time in my entire life I felt my heart and head connect as one and everything I thought I knew flew right out the window with the exhale of my own breath that I didn't even realize I was holding. It was my moment of TRUE salvation. He said it was time to draw a line in the sand and say THIS is where it ends.

I can't keep walking down the same roads as I was before. I cannot pitch my tent in the devil's playground and expect to be ok. I have to set myself apart because God pulled me out and set me free. I am not a slave to evil anymore. Satan has been lying to me about my own salvation. I was saved and baptized a few years ago at a time in my life when I was doing OK. I was on a mountain, but it wasn't long until I slung myself back into the valley and started my path to destruction again. So the devil is using that against me right now and I won't have it. I have questioned it enough since coming here to Jacob's Well so TODAY I am going to reclaim my well earned title as the daughter of a King.

Jesus Christ gave up His whole life so that I could live and I refuse to live it the way I have been. I say again today that Jesus Christ is the Son of God, he came to the earth, suffered a horrible death, and died on a cross for my sins. He then rose from the dead and is alive today in my heart and at the right hand of God in Heaven. Lord, please forgive me for all the things I have done wrong. Forgive me for my sins, Lord. I am so unworthy for your love, but You love me anyway. I am desperate for you. Today I proclaim, with everything I have in my heart, that Jesus is the Beginning and the End for me. He is the Alpha and the Omega, the Sun in the morning sky, the Rock beneath my feet, the Lamp unto my path, my Best Friend. He is all in me all the time, never will leave me, NEVER forsake me, always loving, always patient, always gentle. A true Gentleman. He is my shield of protection from the enemy who wants me dead - the enemy that almost got his way with my death more than once. Jesus was always there. From this moment forward I have no question and no doubt in my mind which Lord I serve. I will fight the good fight, run steady the race before me, and die trying to please Him and glorify Him in all I do. I am reclaiming my life and my relationship with God.

2 Corinthians 4:7-10, 16-18 – But we have this treasure in jars of clay to show that this all-surpassing power is from God and not from us. We are hard pressed on every side, but not crushed; perplexed, but not in despair; persecuted, but not abandoned; struck down, but not destroyed. We always carry around in our body the death of Jesus, so that the life of Jesus may also be revealed in our body.
Therefore we do not lose heart. Though outwardly we are wasting away, yet inwardly we are being renewed day by day. For our light and momentary troubles are achieving for us an eternal glory that far outweighs them all. So we fix our eyes not on what is seen, but on what is unseen, since what is seen is temporary, but what is unseen is eternal.

4 – Words of the Heart

July 9th – 2013 - Day 44 - I am halfway to the halfway point of this journey. The battle I have been in this past week has been crazy. I am so worried about finances, my husband's comings and goings, and I am still judging every single person that I come in contact with. What in the world is really going on?? Do I trust people in my life? Not yet, but I trust my Father. And then I prayed...and then I was shown that I move too fast. I already knew THAT.

I am still trying to run the show and it's making me miserable. Even when I am trying to remain calm and positive, it's from my own strength and not Gods. It's wearing me out, and that is what is about to take me out. This is silly of me. I NEED TO SIT STILL. And breathe. I need to stop speaking so negatively about people and to people and even over my own life. Susan's devotion yesterday really struck a chord with me. Here is what I took away from it:

Proverbs 18:20-21 – From the fruit of their mouth a person's stomach is filled; with the harvest of their lips they are satisfied. The tongue has the power of life and death, and those who love it will eat its fruit.

I can speak life over myself and others or I can speak death. The choice is mine. Through my words I have the power to change my circumstances!

Proverbs 10:11 – The mouth of the righteous is a fountain of life, but the mouth of the wicked conceals violence.

I don't want to be wicked anymore. To even think that my words conceal violence does not line up with my heart at ALL. That is just not OK.

Mark 11:23 – "Truly I tell you, if anyone says to this mountain, 'Go, throw yourself into the sea,' and does not doubt in their heart but believes that what they say will happen, it will done for them."

God can do anything as long as I believe, I don't hold a grudge against anyone else, as long as my motives are pure and not selfish, and if my desire will benefit the kingdom of God. Then my mountains will move!! Checking myself and my list of "NEEDS" will really put things in perspective. I need faith in God, not faith in the object of my request! THAT'S DEEP STUFF!!!

Matthew 12:36-37 – But I tell you that everyone will have to give account on the day of judgment for every empty word they have spoken. For by your words you will be acquitted, and by your words you will be condemned.

WOW. I have a lot to be accountable for at the day of judgment, but if my WORDS can send me to hell, then I have a lot of confessing to do. Susan said, "Out of the overflow of the heart, the mouth speaks." I know my heart, and I know my words are NOT matching up. I can't solve my heart problem by myself. I need the Holy Spirit (The Spirit of Jesus) to fill me up with a new attitude. Susan said I need to have a desire to change, I need to stop making excuses because excuses are nails that build a house of failure. I need to take immediate action and do something I have never been willing to do before. Procrastination stops change. I must change how I see myself. When I have nothing to hide, I hide nothing. I must NEVER go back to the way things were. And most important, I need to STOP waiting for someone else to do it for me. I can change me, no one else can change me but ME and God is my source of the power to change. Change begins with my words, words I speak about myself, about others, about my situations. And words begin with a thought... If you don't think the Lord speaks through His Word, check this out. That same night that Susan did her devotion, Brother Ray did his and followed up with these verses:

Matthew 7:1 – Do not judge, or you will be judged. 1 Timothy 6:8 – But if we have food and clothing, we will be content with that. Hebrews 13:5 – Keep your lives free from the love of money and be content with what you have, because God has said, "never will I leave you; never will I forsake you."

The Lord was speaking to me. Let Him speak to you! It's there for the taking! His Word is ALIVE and TRUE!!

5 – Finding Peace

It's the first week of July, I'm over my 3o day hump, and my relationship with my husband is in constant turmoil. Everything is filled with discord. It's obvious that I have a control problem. I don't understand what he is going through out in the real world nor do I really care. That is a sad reminder of my selfishness. I'm just at a loss. He is going through his own battles and his own struggles with the reality of our situation. He is also just starting a new job, looking for a place to live, trying to handle the finances, and dealing with me being gone. He is also trying to come to terms with his salvation and walk it out with fear and trembling. I should have more empathy, but I am still angry with the way things went down and I hold a lot bitterness and resentment. I really just want to throw in the towel. I am looking for some peace.

God's Word is my answer to peace. I should not give up, I need to GROW UP.

Lord, please deliver me from this bondage. I am stuck. I am angry and upset. Doesn't he see why I don't trust him? Why can't he own up to his stuff? Why does this all fall on me? Lord, please show me what I need to see in myself. Please show me what needs to be worked on today in ME.

John 16:33 – I have told you these things, so that in me you may have peace. In this world you will have trouble. But take heart! I have overcome the world!

This verse was given to me TWICE TODAY. Jesus has overcome the world! Isn't there peace in that?

John 14:27 – Peace I leave with you; my peace I give you. I do not give to you as the world gives. Do not let your hearts be troubled and do not be afraid.

If I get the idea in my head that everything concerning me and my circumstances and relationships should always be perfect, I am setting myself up for a fall. All the mishaps in the world cannot harm me if I will remain in the love of God, displaying the fruit of the spirit.

Galatians 5:22-23 – But the fruit of the Spirit is love, joy, peace, forbearance, kindness, goodness, faithfulness, gentleness and self-control. Against such things there is no law.

God offers Peace when restlessness surrounds me. Peace with God is confident assurance in ANY and ALL circumstances. It is irreplaceable confidence!!

Matthew 6:31-34 – "So do not worry, saying, 'What shall we eat?' or 'What shall we drink?' or 'What shall we wear?' For the pagans run after all these things, and your heavenly Father knows that you need them. But seek first his kingdom and his righteousness, and all these things will be given to you as well. Therefore do not worry about tomorrow, for tomorrow will worry about itself. Each day has enough trouble of its own."

TRUST GOD ONE DAY AT A TIME, one minute at a time, one second at a time. He will move mountains. I can remove bitterness from my life by honestly expressing my feelings to God, forgiving those who have wronged me, and being content with what I have. I need to see that time away from my husband will allow the bitter wounds to heal. Peace comes when I surrender.

6 – Battle for Deliverance

July 11th – 2013 – Day 46 - Today is Thursday, a day I will never forget as long as I live. Chains that had held me bound for nearly 20 years fell off today. I experienced God in a way I never have before and I finally feel free. Last night was HORRIBLE. satan is such a deceiver that he tries to get to me when I am unconscious and asleep. Last night, it worked. When I woke up this morning, I had so much fear, anxiety, worry, paranoia, and confusion on me that I couldn't even breathe. I was ready to walk out of Jacob's Well. I couldn't stop shaking, and I couldn't stop crying. It was so painful. I soon found out why. My deliverance was coming and Satan wanted me on the plank and out the before that could happen.

Ephesians 6:12 – For our struggle is not against flesh and blood, but against the rulers, against the authorities, against the powers of this dark world and against the spiritual forces of evil in the heavenly realms.

I had the amazing opportunity to sit with Pastor and Mrs. Tilghman today for intense counseling and prayer. I was in prayer with them for over 2 hours and it felt like minutes. God spoke to me. ALL I HAD TO DO WAS LISTEN. Listen to His voice, slow down my thinking, and pay attention to who He was telling me I was. I came to the realization that it isn't all about me. I learned that God knows what He is doing and sometimes it's none of my business. Even if it is horrible at the time, like losing a parent to prison or to suicide, He works all things out for His good. I look at my life when my 1st dad was around. It was chaotic, it was stressful, I hardly ever saw him. I wonder what my life would have been like had he lived. Not just for me, but for the rest of my family. I was 15 years old when he died. I took his death, victimized myself, and CHOSE to walk a different path. I didn't see the big picture. My mom is so happy today. I have an amazing dad who loves me very much and would do anything for me and my sister and his two daughters. He is a provider. He isn't selfish. He loves the Lord with all his heart. And he adores my mom. The reason I fell apart from my family was MY choice. From my family, from my ex-husband, from my own children, all because I was the victim and I was stuck in satan's lies. THE LORD ALLOWED THINGS TO TAKE PLACE SO THAT IN THE END I WOULD GLORIFY HIM THROUGH IT.

Genesis 50:20 – You intended to harm me, but God intended it for good to accomplish what is now being done, the saving of many lives.

The test hurts, and I was in a test for a long time. But it is now my TESTIMONY!!! Jesus will never forsake me in my weakness. He will never leave me. Even when I was making bad choices and near death, He was with me. It was the things I was holding onto that were keeping me sick. This is what I hold onto today:

Romans 8:28-38 – And we know that in all things God works for the good of those who love him, who have been called according to his purpose. For those God foreknew he also predestined to be conformed to the image of his Son, that he might be the firstborn among many brothers and sisters. And those he predestined, he also called; those he called, he also justified; those he justified, he also glorified. What, then, shall we say in response to these things? If God is for us, who can be against us? He who did not spare his own Son, but gave him up for us all – how will he not also, along with him, graciously give us all things? Who will bring

any charge against those whom God has chosen? It is God who justifies. Who then is the one who condemns? No one. Christ Jesus who died – more than that, who was raised to life – is at the right hand of God and is also interceding for us. Who shall separate us from the love of Christ? Shall trouble or hardship or persecution or famine or nakedness or danger or sword? As it is written: "For your sake we face death all day long; we are considered as sheep to be slaughtered." NO, IN ALL THESE THINGS WE ARE MORE THAN CONQUERORS THROUGH HIM WHO LOVED US. FOR I AM CONVINCED THAT NEITHER DEATH NOR LIFE, NEITHER ANGELS NOR DEMONS, NEITHER THE PRESENT NOR THE FUTURE, NOR ANY POWERS, NEITHER HEIGHT NOR DEPTH, NOR ANYTHING ELSE IN ALL CREATION, WILL BE ABLE TO SEPARATE US FROM THE LOVE OF GOD THAT IS IN CHRIST JESUS OUR LORD.

Today, I was delivered and set free. I saw the truth. I heard the Lord tell me that I had a purpose. I heard Him say that He was turning every bad circumstance in my life around for His good. He knew me before I was born and even knitted me in my mother's womb. He knew every bad thing that would happen to me and every bad choice I would make. I have a new mind-set and a new perspective now. I learned to accept, not resent, pain and persecution. He has always known me and His love has never failed. It is IMPOSSIBLE to be separated from Christ!! Today I was called out of my pit of shame, guilt and remorse, and I was called into the loving arms of my Savior! I still miss my dad very much, and today I can say that I am GRATEFUL for ALL of it, the good, the bad, and the ugly!! I finally choose to put the past where it belongs and stop fighting a battle that was never mine to fight.

7 – *Self-Reliance*

July 12th – 2013 - Day 47 - Someone once told me that self-reliance is self-destruction. That is more than true for me. I have always had to rely on myself and I always was destructive. I was so deep in addiction, that no one that truly cared about me wanted anything to do with me. I had to find my own way and that wasn't easy. Even in my first few months at Jacob's Well, I was running on my own strength and let me tell you, it was EXHAUSTING. It took a long time for me to lay down all my struggles and allow God to do His work. God is, and must be, my answer to every question and cry of need. Otherwise, I will continue to my path of self-destruction. God can call us in the middle of our present obedience if we are doing His will, His way, and in His strength – not ours. For me, I like to prepare. I like well-layed out plans; I don't do well in chaotic environments. However, I have learned to adapt to those types of environments and pray through it all because otherwise I will start to run on my own and forget that God is in control. Did I mention that I was a control freak? Gideon, an Israelite, was minding his own business, doing what he had to do just to survive by hiding his work of threshing wheat in a winepress to keep it from the Midianites who would steal the wheat if they saw him doing it. Just doing his task. He believed that his clan was the weakest in Manasseh and he believed he was the weakest in his family. That doesn't really give him a head start does it? He already thinks he is the weakest person in his ENTIRE CLAN. Wow. Sounds familiar. But guess who God called to go deliver all of Israel out of the hands of the Midianites? Gideon! So Gideon takes 32,000 men to fight a huge battle. That's only fair, right?

Judges 7:2 – The Lord said to Gideon, "You have too many men. I cannot deliver Midian into their hands, or Israel would boast against me, 'My own strength has saved me.'"

God wanted to prove a point about self-reliance. It is a handicap when it makes me believe that I can do whatever needs to get done in my own strength. I need to be sure to give God the credit for ALL my victories. Complacency is DANGER...DANGER...DANGER and it makes me forget that I am just Julie, and GOD IS GOD.

Judges 7:8 – So Gideon sent the rest of the Israelites home but kept the three hundred, who took over the provisions and trumpets of the others.

God took 32,000 and weeded them down to 300! The Bible says the Midiantes were so numerous that they were thick as locusts and their camel could no more be counted than the sand on the seashore (Judges 7:12)! I would be shaking in my boots and running away if I were Gideon, but he relied on the strength of the LORD. All Gideon and his men had to do was blow some trumpets and break some jars and the Midianites turned on themselves. That is a Mighty God and all He wanted was the glory! If Gideon had gone in his own might, in his own way, with his own plan, he wouldn't have survived and Israel would have fallen.

Isaiah 33:10 – "Now will I arise", says the Lord. "Now will I be exalted; now will I be lifted up."

God is stepping in and taking over. He is sick of the hot air that I blow and sick of me self-destructing. Fine by me! The kicker...I must LET HIM! I must allow Him to weed out the army I think I have. I must follow His guidelines (THE BIBLE) because all He is doing is protecting me from myself and from my own consequences.

1 Corinthians 1:27 – But God chose the foolish things of the world to shame the wise; God chose the weak things of the world to shame the strong. 2 Corinthians 12:9 – But he said to me, "My grace is sufficient for you, for my power is made perfect in weakness." Therefore I will boast all the more gladly about my weaknesses, so that Christ's power may rest on me.

Christ is my strength. I can't fight these battles alone.

8 – *Pruning the Branch of Perfection*

July 18th – 2013 – Day 54 - I managed the Corner Store today. Mrs. Mandy asked me to clean the shelves and move some things around. It was a pretty simple request but obviously not for me. Because of my strange need for perfection, I took it to a whole new level and completely freaked out the girl who was working with me. Before, I wouldn't have cared, but I did not like the look of fear and worry on her face and in her countenance. I knew it was because of my perfectionism. That hurt me to know I did that to her. I realized today that my need for perfection comes from my 1st dad. He was always seeking perfection and he fell because of it- died for it. That became a branch on my vine that wasn't producing any fruit. That was made obvious by how my words, my negativity, and my unrealistic expectations were causing this girl so much grief. I did a lot of gossiping today, too, and I'm sure that didn't help the situation. I turned to gossip to try to get her out of her own head and that sure didn't work for either of us. I failed today – miserably.

Deuteronomy 5:9-10 – You shall not bow down to them or worship them; for I, the Lord your God, am a jealous God, punishing the children for the sin of the parents to the third and fourth generation of those who hate me, but showing love to a thousand generations of those who love me and keep my commandments.

I also realized that day that the generational curse that was passed to me from my dad was still at large. Even though the Lord had broken those chains regarding his death, I was still holding onto the branch on the vine that wasn't doing so well that season. I was still worshiping little gods that I didn't even know existed -

Pride, gossip, and perfection - funny how those things can just sneak right up on me.

Psalm 79:8 – Do not hold against us the sins of past generations; may your mercy come quickly to meet us, for we are in desperate need.

I don't want this on me anymore. I don't want to suffer and in turn cause others to suffer. It's time to cut off the branch that isn't bearing fruit. Asa always says there has to be a level of maturity in my everyday walk and I am not being mature when I am putting others down in order to deflect my own issues. Hopefully, God will honor my humility and my reality.

John 15:1-5 - "I am the true vine, and my Father is the gardener. He cuts off every branch in me that bears no fruit, while every branch that does bear fruit he prunes so that it will be even more fruitful. You are already clean because of the word I have spoken to you. Remain in me, as I also remain in you. No branch can bear fruit by itself; it must remain in the vine. Neither can you bear fruit unless you remain in me. I am the vine, you are the branches. If you remain in me and I in you, you will bear much fruit; apart from me you can do nothing."

I can allow God to snip my branches back and I can check myself for my own attitude in situations, negative talk, gossip, and perfection and allow Him to do His work in me. I can allow God to cut back the branches and allow new growth through discipline in order to strengthen my character, or I can allow him to CUT IT OFF completely because it is worthless to the vine and is infecting the rest of the tree. Now, this also symbolizes my walk with the Lord. Jesus is the vine, and I am the branch. If I am not bearing good fruit, I will be cut off from His life-giving power. I sure don't want THAT. It's past time for a major pruning.

Galatians 5:22-23 - But the fruit of the Spirit is love, joy, peace, forbearance, kindness, goodness, faithfulness, gentleness and self-control. Against such things there is no law.

9 – The "Fake it 'til You Make It" Lie

Every time I have ever been to a treatment facility, I went in with a plan. I was always there to please someone else and my plan was to always fake it until I made it, get a good grade, and get out of there. Granted, there were times in my life where being clean and staying clean were a top priority, but never for the right reasons. I never recognized my true weaknesses: trying to get ahead of others, being jealous of what others had, putting too much stock in temporary benefits, and always seeking approval of others. That is exactly what satan wanted.

If I fake it until I make it, then I will be sure to throw myself back into the pit of guilt, shame, and remorse and start all over again where I left off. A shooting star only lasts for a brief moment before it falls again. I went into most of those treatment centers with an attitude of "I've got this, I'm better than these people!". And that is truly how I felt at Jacob's Well, too, until I realized:

July 19th – 2013 – Day 55 – I am no longer feeling like a fake. I KNOW this is who I am. I am a daughter of the KING. I have believed that from the beginning but there has always been a nagging voice telling me that I was full of it and I listened to that voice. This morning, I learned to accept myself where I am and I am choosing today not to focus on how far I have to go, only in how far I have come. I will no longer compare myself to others. My situation is mine and it is grave unless I finally make a choice to do something different. I am not weak, so I don't need to fake ANYTHING. I have lost my entire life, only to regain it in Christ Jesus!!

Romans 12:9 – Love must be sincere. Hate what is evil; cling to what is good. Matthew 10:39 –

Whoever finds their life will lose it, and whoever loses their life for my sake will find it.

I wasn't willing to give up ANYTHING. It was taken from me because of my bad choices. I was forced to loosen my grip on earthly rewards because there was nothing left to hold onto. I had given it all away for my own selfish desires. It was then that I became truly free. Free to follow Christ. I went to last place. I stopped trying to be at the top of the ladder (most days that was a REAL struggle for me), and I started truly following Jesus. I became willing to make sacrifices for greater rewards later, even if they DIDN'T come when I thought they should.

Matthew 19:30 – But many who are first will be last, and many who are last will be first.

I have God's approval and that is all I need! God will give me favor with Him and with others if I will just do things His way. NO MORE FAKING IT. Jesus is the real deal and He is the only way to achieve true peace and happiness!

TEN – *False Evidence Appearing Real*

Fear – False Evidence Appearing Real. Fear is an emotion induced by a perceived threat which causes entities to quickly pull far away from it and usually hide. Fear is giving into the satan by saying you believe what he is going to accomplish, not what the Lord will accomplish.

I had a lot of fears. I was a genuine "future-tripper". In a sick way, I enjoyed those trips into the future; the planning, the projecting, the anxiety, the worry, the doubt - in a way, it gave me hope - FALSE hope. When my "future-tripping" plans didn't work out the way I wanted, I would end up paralyzed by fear. I was always living in the past and thinking about the future. I was never in the here and now. And it was ALL an illusion.

Living in fear caused me so much stress and worry that I would lash out at anyone around me and try to control every single aspect of my life in order to feel sane again. Prime example:

July 23rd – 2013 - Day 58 - What a day. I was backup at the Corner Store today and was looking forward to relaxing and not making any decisions and things were going great, then...WHAM. Someone asked me about the boys and when they were coming to visit and there went my whole day. I was racked by fear and anxiety. I know they won't be here to see me. When will I ever get to see them? Will I even have the opportunity to talk to them this year? How will I ever pay my debt to them and their parents? I feel completely out of control. I ended up throwing a box on the floor and freaking out on my co-worker and friend. The one thing I can't control came from left field and I tried to take control of everything and everyone else around me when it wasn't my place. DISASTER! Crash and burn!! I was rude, obnoxious, controlling, sad, and I made others around me miserable. Lord, help me see Your way through this fear.

1 John 4:17-19 – 17 This is how love is made complete among us so that we will have confidence on the day of judgment: In this world we are like Jesus. 18 There is no fear in love. But perfect love drives out fear, because fear has to do with punishment. The one who fears is not made perfect in love. 19 We love because he first loved us.

I temporarily lost sight of who I was, THAT DAY. I was looking at all the evidence around me from the past and started looking to the unforeseen future and forgot to focus on Jesus, the perfect example of perfect love. God sent Jesus, a man without sin, to hang on a cross so that I could live without fear. Today I will have courage, and take that step past fear into my destiny.

Isaiah 43:1b-7 – 1b "Do not fear, for I have redeemed you; I have summoned you by name; you are mine. 2 When you pass through the waters, I will be with you; and when you pass through the rivers, they will not sweep over you. When you walk through the fire, you will not be burned; the flames will not set you ablaze. 3 For I am the Lord your God, the Holy One of Israel, your Savior; I give Egypt for your ransom, Cush and Seba in your stead. 4 Since you are precious and honored in my sight, and because I love you, I will give people in exchange for you, nations in exchange for your life. 5 Do not be afraid, for I am with you; I will bring your children from the east and gather you from the west. 6 I will say to the north, 'Give them up!' and to the south, 'Do not hold them back.' Bring my

sons from afar and my daughters from the ends of the earth."

11 – *The Lady at the Well*

July 24th – 2013 – Day 59 - Jesus spoke to me. He showed me who I was and He took the time to sweetly and gently show me who HE was and what He alone could do for me. Just like He did with the woman at Jacob's Well in the Bible.

I was alone, I was scared, I was hopeless, I was helpless, I was near death, I was doing terrible things, I was a victim of my own circumstances, I was sinning, I was LOST – a dead woman walking. I was hungry, I was thirsty, I was tired. Then He rescued me and brought me to my own Jacob's Well where I found healing and comfort. This story makes me cry every time I read it. It touches me on so many levels that it's hard to even find words for it:

John 4:6-26 - 6Jacob's well was there, and Jesus, tired as he was from the journey, sat down by the well. It was about noon. 7 When a Samaritan woman came to draw water, Jesus said to her, "Will you give me a drink?" 8 (His disciples had gone into the town to buy food.) 9 The Samaritan woman said to him, "You are a Jew and I am a Samaritan woman. How can you ask me for a drink?" (For Jews do not associate with Samaritans.) 10 Jesus answered her, "If you knew the gift of God and who it is that asks you for a drink, you would have asked him and he would have given you living water." 11 "Sir," the woman said, "you have nothing to draw with and the well is deep. Where can you get this living water? 12 Are you greater than our father Jacob, who gave us the well and drank from it himself, as did also his sons and his livestock?" 13 Jesus answered, "Everyone who drinks this water will be thirsty again, 14 but whoever drinks the water I give them will never thirst. Indeed, the water I give them will become in them a spring of water welling up to eternal life." 15 The woman said to him, "Sir, give me this water so that I won't get thirsty and have to keep coming here to draw water." 16 He told her, "Go, call your husband and come back." 17 "I have no husband," she replied. Jesus said to her, "You are right when you say you have no husband. 18 The fact is, you have had five husbands, and the man you now have is not your husband. What you have just said is quite true." 19 "Sir," the woman said, "I can see that you are a prophet. 20 Our ancestors worshiped on this mountain, but you Jews claim that the place where we must worship is in Jerusalem." 21 "Woman," Jesus replied, "believe me, a time is coming when you will worship the Father neither on this mountain nor in Jerusalem. 22 You Samaritans worship what you do not know; we worship what we do know, for salvation is from the Jews. 23 Yet a time is coming and has now come when the true worshipers will worship the Father in the Spirit and in truth, for they are the kind of worshipers the Father seeks. 24 God is spirit, and his worshipers must worship in the Spirit and in truth." 25 The woman said, "I know that Messiah" (called Christ) "is coming. When he comes, he will explain everything to us." 26 Then Jesus declared, "I, the one speaking to you—I am he."

I am in my room all by myself at Jacob's Well, rocking on my little bed asking over and over again "Why me?" Tears are falling from my face and I am feeling completely unworthy of anyone's love. Here I am again, back in treatment again; something is different this time, I just can't put my finger on it. The room is dark, but for the light coming from the window next to my bed. I am ashamed, guilt-ridden, alone, and confused.

It's just me and my thoughts. Then I feel a presence next to me. It is Jesus. His warm arms wrap around me so tight.

I look up and He is crying, too, because He feels my hurt and He knows my heart. He begins to offer me hope. He acknowledges all my sins. At that, I squirm and get ready to run from the room. Instead, I find myself creeping off the bed onto the floor to sit at His feet. Before I can even make thoughts, He answers them. With tears streaming down His face, He begs me to stop fighting and to give into Him. It's all He has ever wanted. All He wants is ME. He then whispers to me as I lay at His feet that it is all going to be OK. He will feed me with His Word, He will offer me drink from His fountain. I will never be hungry or thirsty again and my soul will be satisfied. He promises me that He has been there all along and has never left my side and I believe Him. I am filled with a presence and a peace like no other. I look up and I am alone in my dark room again, on the floor.

There is no one around, but I am not alone.

THE I AM IS STILL WITH ME.

12 – *Following Christ into Ministry*

I remember a day at Jacob's Well, right before I hit 60 days in the program. Our amazing Pastor Charlie came in to speak with us and let us in on how he was led by the Holy Spirit to open Righteous Oaks Recovery Center in Meridian for Men and Jacob's Well Recovery Center in Poplarville for Women. He shared Isaiah 61 with us and I was moved.

I am a bit of a history buff, so I did my research on this after he left that night. In Luke 4:18-19, Jesus quotes Isaiah 61:1-2a. Let me set the stage for you. Jesus is getting ready to start his ministry. He will over the next 3 ½ years reach out to people just like me in a culture that is seemingly just like ours. He will reach out to the sick, the blind, the lame, the tax collectors, the prostitutes, the homeless, the broken hearted and then some.

Jesus went to the synagogue in Nazareth, in **his hometown**. The ruler of the synagogue always laid out the plans for worship **4 or 5 years in advance**. The people would sing and pray and then the scroll would be opened, read, and then interpreted. Jesus walked in that day and was viewed as the visiting rabbi, even though it was his hometown, and was given the honor of reading the scroll. He opened it and read:

Isaiah 61:1-2a - The Spirit of the Sovereign Lord is on me, because the Lord has anointed me to proclaim good news to the poor. He has sent me to bind up the broken hearted, to proclaim freedom for the captives and release from darkness for the prisoners, 2 to proclaim the year of the Lord's favor.

Can you imagine the gasp that must have come from the people when he slowly rolled up the scroll, handed it to the ruler of the synagogue, then calmly sat down and said, "Today this scripture is fulfilled in your hearing." (**Luke 4:21**)? BOOM!!! After reading through the rest of Isaiah 61, I was encouraged to know that Pastor Charlie and his wonderful family (who had all been redeemed from the gates of hell themselves) were starting their own ministry in the wake of what Jesus did. That is just awesome and I am so grateful. If they had not listened to the voice of the Lord, I would not be sitting here writing - I would be six feet under. I hope to follow in the footsteps of Christ one day myself!!!

Isaiah 61:2b-11 - and the day of vengeance of our God, to comfort all who mourn, 3 and provide for those who grieve in Zion— to bestow on them a crown of beauty instead of ashes, the oil of joy instead of mourning, and a garment of praise instead of a spirit of despair. They will be called oaks of righteousness, a planting of the Lord for the display of his splendor. 4 They will rebuild the ancient ruins and restore the places long devastated; they will renew the ruined cities that have been devastated for generations. 5 Strangers will shepherd your flocks; foreigners will work your fields and vineyards. 6 And you will be called priests of the Lord, you will be named ministers of our God. You will feed on the wealth of nations, and in their riches you will boast. 7 Instead of your shame you will receive a double portion, and instead of disgrace you will rejoice in your inheritance. And so you will inherit a double portion in your land, and everlasting joy will be yours. 8 "For I, the Lord, love justice; I hate robbery and wrongdoing. In my faithfulness I will reward my people and make an everlasting covenant with them. 9 Their descendants will be known among the nations and their offspring among the peoples All who see them will acknowledge that they are a people the Lord has blessed." 10 I delight greatly in the Lord; my soul rejoices in my God. For he has clothed me with garments of salvation and arrayed me in a robe of his righteousness, as a bridegroom adorns his head like a priest, and as a bride adorns herself with her jewels. 11 For as the soil makes the sprout come up and a garden causes seeds to grow, so the Sovereign Lord will make righteousness and praise spring up before all nations.

I love the Lord's promises, and there are many in this scripture!! I can't wait to see it all unfold in my life as I do my part to follow His ways in eager anticipation of His glorious return!!

13 – *Using Kid Gloves*

July 26th - 2013 – Day 61 - I love watching the Lord move and listening when He speaks. Today Liz, Susan's daughter, came to the Corner Store to work with us all day. She is such a sweet girl and she blessed me in so many ways today! She is smart as a whip and I got to show her all the workings of the store. We rearranged shelves, made signs, and had a great time. I realized that I was able to teach her stuff without offending her and because of that I am going to change my approach on the way I train people moving forward.

I should no longer assume that people should just know stuff because I do. That in turn upsets them. I didn't upset her today and light bulbs went off. I didn't WANT to offend her and I shouldn't WANT to offend anyone else for that matter. I used kid gloves and so I will do that from this point going forward.

I am so grateful that she was there today even though I was TERRIFIED of her. She taught me more than I could ever teach her. I was a terrible person to learn from. I expected way too much of people and in turn, feelings were hurt, my expectations weren't met, and people wanted nothing to do with me. My entire mindset changed the day I got to teach a 10 year old about how to run the Corner Store. I wasn't expecting too much from her. I just wanted her to enjoy her time and have fun. Isn't that what I would hope for with everyone?

1 Corinthians 15:58 – Therefore, my dear brothers and sisters, stand firm. Let nothing move you. Always give yourselves fully to the work of the Lord, because you know that your labor in the Lord in not in vain.

For me, this means to work as unto the Lord, train as unto the Lord, speak to others as unto the Lord....not as unto Julie.

1 Peter 3:8 – Finally, all of you, be like-minded, be sympathetic, love one another, be compassionate and humble.

Treat others with respect is what I learned from this. Treat them as I would expect to be treated. It's time to put on the kid gloves, humble myself, and allow others to be where they are, not where I expect them to be. Jesus loves them right where they are...why can't I?

14 – OUCH! The Truth Hurts!

July 29th – 2013 – Day 64 - Who am I? What do I stand for? How do others perceive me? Hearing the truth to these questions is sometimes very difficult.

I was so messed up and treated people with no respect, so the answers to the questions were not always what I wanted to hear. I had a real hard time dealing with the truth. But it helped me heal. I am so grateful for honest, caring, uplifting individuals that God placed in my life that told it to me straight. Did I take offense? Sure. But God dealt with me regarding offenses and I was able to see past that into their loving eyes to see they were only trying to help me, not hurt me. I can promise you, that if I don't see the truth and try to work through things, God will deal with me. He always does.

John 8:31-32 – To the Jews who had believed him Jesus said, "If you hold to my teaching, you are really my disciples. 32 Then you will know the truth, and the truth will set you free." Ephesians 4:15 – Instead, speaking the truth in love, we will grow to become in every respect the mature body of him who is the head, that is, Christ.

I want to be mature and I want to be FREE! I feel like I have been stuck in my 16 year old mind for way too long. No wonder I couldn't get it together. I can't grow without the truth. I will still be stuck in my own fantasy world if it weren't for the truth and I would not be moving to a new level in my walk with Christ. He says to speak truth in love. That is what others did for me, and it is what I hope to do with others.

I no longer want to stumble on confrontation and getting all bent out of shape because I don't want to hear what is being said to me, out of love and care. God wants me to get rid of the bad so that I can have what He wants me to have! I am my own stumbling block!!

John 16:13 – But when he, the Spirit of Truth, comes, he will guide you into all the truth. He will not speak on his own; he will speak only what he hears, and he will tell you what is yet to come.

If I don't submit myself to the Lord, then my life will not get any better and I will be stuck with a huge problem, being alone again - not a friend in the world who wants anything to do with my rebellious, stubborn, disobedient, rude, easily offended self. It's time to get real and put on my big girl panties. Time to face the truth.

15 – The Throne Room

July 30th – 2013 - Day 65 - I got a HUGE blessing and a very big revelation today. I got to go to the eye doctor! I used to take things like that for granted. I took everything for granted. Something as simple as getting to go to the eye doctor opened my eyes to the way I used to treat people in all types of business establishments. I was always very rude and very much in a hurry. Not the easiest of clients to say the least.

The people there took very good care of me and I walked out with a new prescription and an order for new glasses. It has been years since I can say I did that for myself and the people of Jacob's Well made it happen for me today. I sat in the office there and cried like a baby - Godly sorrow of how I used to be and how I don't want to be anymore. I am so grateful. What a beautiful gift!

I was then blessed with prayer time with Pastor Tilghman again today. I got to go into a room with him and Josette and quiet my mind long enough to really hear from the Lord. We began to pray and I immediately saw myself at the pool at the Country Club in Ruston, LA. I could hear children playing; I could smell the chlorine in the pool. It represented a day of innocence and joy for me! A day when all things were right in the world.

I was then transported directly into the throne room of heaven! I could feel the loving embrace of my Heavenly Father in this beautiful light. The love in the light was almost too much! Pastor Tilghman began to sing "Sweet Spirit" and I was immediately taken to the memory of me and Papaw and our sportsman day when he taught me how to fish (and not catch squirrels), how to golf (I hit a hole in one on our little makeshift hole in his field), and how to bowl.

Papaw took such good care of me that day and God told me that He takes care of me like that all the time!! He wants me to have perfect days like that and He wants to give me the desires of my heart. I sat in the Glory of the Lord for a long time in prayer and thanksgiving. What a joyous moment and some joyous memories!

I should be able to listen to God's voice until it is the loudest voice I hear. I tend to let the white noise of the world interfere with His still small voice. Being in the presence of the Most High God is the most exhilarating place to be and I can get there anytime I want as long as I am willing to humble myself, quiet my mind, remember His goodness and His promises, and reflect on His grace and mercy. I want to daily claim my new position in Christ and listen to His voice alone.

Elijah was afraid and running for his life away from Jezebel. She was angry with him because he had defeated 850 of the prophets of Baal on Mount Carmel by showing them the One and Only God. Jezebel wanted him dead. He was scared to death so he hid in a cave.

1 Kings 19:9b-13 – And the word of the Lord came to him: "What are you doing here Elijah?" 10 He replied, "I have been very zealous for the Lord God Almighty. The Israelites have rejected your covenant, torn down your altars, and put your prophets to death with the sword. I am the only one left, and now they are trying to kill me too." 11 The Lord said, "Go out and stand on the mountain in the presence of the Lord, for the Lord is about to pass by." Then a great and powerful wind tore the mountains apart and shattered the rocks before the Lord, but the Lord was not in the wind. After the wind there was an earthquake, but the Lord was not in the earthquake. 12 After the earthquake came a fire, but the Lord was not in the fire. And after the fire came a gentle whisper. 13 When Elijah heard it, he pulled his cloak over his face and went out and stood at the mouth of the cave.

The Lord is ALWAYS passing by, and He comes not with pomp and circumstance, but in a gentle whisper. I am ready to meet Him on the mountain, I am ready to meet Him in the throne room, and I am ready to meet Him in heaven. I just have to open my spiritual ears to hear his still, small voice. He will whisper in the quietness of a humbled heart!!

Psalm 145:18 – The Lord is near to all who call on him, to all who call on him in truth.

16 – *Becoming De-Institutionalized*

Psalm 20:4 – May he give you the desire of your heart and make all your plans succeed.

God is definitely in the miracle business and I have seen it in my life firsthand. Being homeless wasn't easy OR fun, nor was being institutionalized.

One of the definitions of "institutionalize" as per Webster is to accustom (a person) so firmly to the care and supervised routine of an institution as to make incapable of managing a life outside.

I was definitely incapable of managing life. I was always told I had a disease and I was told by some people that I would never get well and I was told that I wasn't worth it. I know people who go back to jail time and time again because it's comfortable for them. They find ways to mess up (sometimes subconsciously) because in jail there is nothing to worry about; no bills to pay, no mouths to feed, no real worries at all. They are fed everyday like clockwork and have a bed to sleep in. They don't learn how to work for themselves nor do they feel worthy of anything great. They can't see the forest for the trees. It was the same for me in treatment centers. I wasn't there for the right reasons.

People in jail and treatment either get it or they don't. I am not saying this about everyone or every institution. It depends on the person there. There are many different ways to be institutionalized; jails, treatment centers, shelters, hospitals. The worst type of institution for me was behind my eyeballs in my own mind. It's a terrible and terrifying feeling being stuck in the "I Can't(s)". Here is the good news: GOD CAN, He will, and He does!

August 8th – 2013 – Day 74 off the streets, out of my head, and in the comfortable and loving arms of Jesus - I have always been in control (or what I portrayed as being in control). Being here at Jacob's Well has forced me to step out of my comfort zone and allow God to be in control. I'm not going to lie, most days it sucks. I know my own thinking got me where I am today so why not let Jesus take the wheel? Today, He showed me what He could do when I let go and let God. To say this week has been filled with panic is an understatement. When I lose control, I act out, so I'm sure I haven't been a pleasure to be around. I felt like leaving this week so I could go "Fix-It". Yeah, right. Like that's worked before. It has been 13 years since I can say I had a place of my own; a place where I could REALLY contribute. I have paid rent elsewhere, but it was never mine. I've lived with my parents, been in jail, been in hospitals, been in shelters, been trapped in my mind on the street, had rent paid for me, lived in recovery homes, lived with friends....NEVER a place of my own. God's angels intervened today and due to what only God could do, I have a home to go to when I leave here. I am no longer institutionalized. I AM FREE!!!

Psalm 40:1-3 – I waited patiently for the Lord; he turned to me and heard my cry. 2 He lifted me up out of the slimy pit, out of the mud and mire; he set my feet on a rock and gave me a firm place to stand. 3 He put a new song in my mouth, a hymn of praise to our God. Many will see and fear the Lord and put their trust in Him.

God is trustworthy. He is faithful. He is true. And He wants to give me the desires of my heart. All I have to do is put it all in His hands!!

1 Peter 5:6-11 – Humble yourselves, therefore, under God's mighty hand, that he may lift you up in due

time. 7 Cast all your anxiety on him because he cares for you. 8 Be alert and of sober mind. Your enemy the devil prowls around like a roaring lion looking for someone to devour. 9 Resist him, standing firm in the faith, because you know that the family of believers throughout the world is undergoing the same kind of sufferings. 10 And the God of all grace, who called you to his eternal glory in Christ, after you have suffered a little while, will himself restore you and make you strong, firm and steadfast. 11 To him be the power forever and ever. Amen.

My anxieties took a backseat to the miracle that took place that day. God called me out of my sin and into his glory in Christ and He blessed me. What a good Daddy!

Jeremiah 31:3 – The Lord appeared to us in the past, saying: "I have loved you with an everlasting glove; I have drawn you with unfailing kindness."

God speaks. God moves. Nothing in heaven or on earth can stop His plan for my life! I must be willing to listen, and do whatever is required and I will drink from a fountain that will never run dry.

17 – *Obedience*

August 17th – 2013 - Day 83 - I worked at the Corner Store today (Jacob's Well Thrift Grocery Store). It was my last month of food stamps and I went to town buying everything under the sun for snacks. I have been without, so I racked up and was so proud of my loot! I got back home (to Jacob's Well), unpacked it all, and stood back admiring my purchases. For once, I wasn't going to have to wait until someone offered me something. I had it all to myself! THEN - the Lord quickly told me to look at it and admire it, but to give it ALL away.

I knew for sure it wasn't my voice I was listening to, so I battled with Him right there in my room. I questioned it over and over. I thought long and hard about it. I pondered it. Then I begrudgingly obeyed my Master. I sought out Tammy (our house mom) and told her what had just taken place. After she had a good laugh, she asked me who I wanted to give it to. I let her pick. She chose the 3 girls in the house that I had the biggest problems with. Go figure! God sure does have a sense of humor.

I got three grocery bags and divided my precious snacks up. Needless to say, I didn't like doing it, but I couldn't go against the nagging feeling in my soul that it was the right thing to do. Obedience is tough for this gal. I finally started submitting myself to what it was that God wanted me to do. Did I do it every day? No. Did it mean I was happy about it? No. Did it mean that I did it willingly all the time? No. But I DID DO IT. And I still do it. Are there are still some things in my life I am holding onto? Yes. I hold onto my things, my habits, my emotions, and my stuff in general like they are long lost friends who I don't want to say goodbye to again. And it isn't healthy. Am I convicted in my heart on these things on a daily basis? Yes. Do I need to start obeying? Yes. God has been talking about obedience since Genesis and the creation of man. When I am obedient, even in the small things (like giving up my little possessions), then I will be blessed and those blessings will OVERFLOW to others – today and into eternity. Jesus himself had to learn about obedience. We know from scripture that He begged God to not allow him to die such a horrible death.

Hebrews 5:8-9 – Son though he was, he learned obedience from what he suffered 9 and, once made perfect, he became the source of eternal salvation for all who obey him.

If Jesus is willing to die on a cross by obeying the will of God, then what am I complaining about when He asks me to give up something so small as a piece of beef jerky? Hmmmm….

Romans 8:16-18 – Don't you know that when you offer yourselves to someone as obedient slaves, you are slaves of the one you obey – whether you are slaves to sin, which leads to death, or to obedience, which leads to righteousness? 17 But thanks be to God that, though you used to be slaves to sin, you have come to obey from your heart the pattern of teaching that has now claimed your allegiance. 18 You have been set free from sin and have become slaves to righteousness.

What I do, how I act, and the little things I hold on to have Jesus shaking his head at me. I can be a slave to my little things, emotions, and habits; or, I can be a slave to obedience to Jesus and in turn claim my new allegiance. Obedience brings blessings beyond my wildest imaginations!!

18 – *Purposed for Change*

August 25th – 2013 – 90 Days - I used to go in and out of treatment centers with the best of intentions (or so I thought). In reality, I was really only trying to please those around me and I hurt everyone in the process. It never stuck. I would stay clean for a while and then I was back off the races. Until August 25th, 2013, I had never done anything for my recovery on purpose and because I really wanted to. I had never stayed anywhere for that long with the HONEST intentions of doing something different.

August 25th used to carry meaning for me in a negative way. It was the day my dad committed suicide and the day satan lied to me and told me that it was my fault. The great deceiver told me that I would be just like my dad. I WAS just like him and I almost met the same fate as him more than once. I THANK GOD every day for my new life in Christ Jesus and that I am not six feet under by my own hand. When the Lord spoke to me about what I should say in church service on August 25th, 2013, He spoke to me about deliverance, obedience, transformation, and restoration. I will carry what I learned at Jacob's Well with me for the rest of my life and I am so grateful.   I am no longer bound by the chains of my father's mistakes. I am free of that generational curse and I will never look back because I want my own children to be free. August 25th will forever carry a positive meaning for me. It was the day I decided to truly commit myself to the program there and follow through with whatever God would have me do from now until eternity!!

Psalm 116 – I love the Lord, for he heard my voice; he heard my cry for mercy. 2 Because he turned his ear to me, I will call on him as long as I live. 3 The

cords of death entangled me, the anguish of the grave came over me; I was overcome by distress and sorrow. 4 Then I called on the name of the Lord: "Lord, save me!" 5 The Lord is gracious and righteous; our God is full of compassion. 6 The Lord protects the unwary; when I was brought low, he saved me. 7 Return to your rest, my soul, for the Lord has been good to you. 8 For you, Lord, have delivered me from death, my eyes from tears, my feet from stumbling, 9 that I may walk before the Lord in the land of the living. 10 I trusted in the Lord when I said, "I am greatly afflicted"; 11 in my alarm I said, "Everyone is a liar." 12 What shall I return to the Lord for all his goodness to me? 13 I will lift up the cup of salvation and call on the name of the Lord. 14 I will fulfill my vows to the Lord in the presence of all his people. 15 Precious in the sight of the Lord is the death of his faithful servants. 16 Truly I am your servant, Lord; I serve you just as my mother did; you have freed me from my chains. 17 I will sacrifice a thank offering to you and call on the name of the Lord. 18 I will fulfill my vows to the Lord in the presence of all his people, 19 in the courts of the house of the Lord – in your midst, Jerusalem. PRAISE BE THE LORD.

I wanted to change so bad I could taste it. I was tired of living the life I was in and I knew that something had to give or I was going to die lonely, miserable, and afraid. The story of Rahab inspired me to do something different, to see past my PAST and look toward my purpose.

Rahab was a prostitute in Jericho. She was a sneaky little thing, living on the edge of society, one heartbeat away from total rejection (sounds familiar). She was singled out by the Israelite spies before God had the walls of Jericho fall to His chosen people led by Joshua.

Rahab lived IN the wall of Jericho. Her house was built right into the side of it. She had a front row seat to the workings of the whole city at her front door and the much discussed encroaching Israelites at her back door. Opportunity knocked and she answered! She had turned to God for salvation and He granted it to her and in the process spoke to her heart regarding the spies that had their own agenda as to why they came to her for refuge.

Joshua 2:8-21 - Before the spies lay down for the night, she went up on the roof 9 and said to them, "I know that the Lord has given you this land and that a great fear of you has fallen on us, so that all who live in this country are melting in fear because of you. 10 We have heard how the Lord dried up the water of the Red Sea for you when you came out of Egypt, and what you did to Sihon and Og, the two kings of the Amorites east of the Jordan, whom you completely destroyed. 11 When we heard of it, our hearts melted in fear and everyone's courage failed because of you, for the Lord your God is God in heaven above and on the earth below. 12 "Now then, please swear to me by the Lord that you will show kindness to my family, because I have shown kindness to you. Give me a sure sign 13 that you will spare the lives of my father and mother, my brothers and sisters, and all who belong to them— and that you will save us from death." 14 "Our lives for your lives!" the men assured her. "If you don't tell what we are doing, we will treat you kindly and faithfully when the Lord gives us the land." 15 So she let them down by a rope through the window, for the house she lived in was part of the city wall. 16 She said to them, "Go to the hills so the pursuers will not find you. Hide yourselves there three days until they return, and then go on your way." 17 Now the men had said to her, "This

*oath you made us swear will not be binding on us
18 unless, when we enter the land, you have tied
this scarlet cord in the window through which you
let us down, and unless you have brought your
father and mother, your brothers and all your
family into your house. 19 If any of them go outside
your house into the street, their blood will be on
their own heads; we will not be responsible. As for
those who are in the house with you, their blood
will be on our head if a hand is laid on them. 20
But if you tell what we are doing, we will be
released from the oath you made us swear." 21
"Agreed," she replied. "Let it be as you say." So she
sent them away, and they departed. And she tied
the scarlet cord in the window.*

Rahab desired a change and she positioned herself for
that change. My past behavior does NOT disqualify me
from being used by God. First, though, I need to allow
God to shine the light of Truth on my life so that I can
see things more clearly and ask for forgiveness. Even
when I am broken and beat down, God is always
prepared to send someone to come along and encourage
me.

When the wall of Jericho fell, Rahab's house remained
standing...the only part of the wall that continued to
exist. That woman saved by Grace, purposed for a new
life, became the mother of Boaz who was the great-
grandfather to King David who was the ancestor of
Jesus Christ Himself! She was purposed by God and
her past mistakes could not haunt her any longer!

*2 Corinthians 4:7-10 – But we have this treasure in
jars of clay to show that this all-surpassing power
is from God and not from us. 8 We are hard pressed
on every side, but not crushed; perplexed, but not in
despair; 9 persecuted, but not abandoned; struck*

down, but not destroyed. 10 We always carry around in our body the death of Jesus, so that the life of Jesus may also be revealed in our body.

Purpose YOURSELF for change and let God do His Mighty Work in YOU!

19 – *Being OK in Second Place*

Have you ever been picked second or even last for something? It reminds me of being on the playground as a kid. I would be standing in a line with the rest of the kids, my fingers crossed behind my back, praying not to be picked last for dodge ball during recess. I wasn't the most athletic in my group of playmates, AND I am a girl, so I usually got picked last for teams. It was humiliating. It stirred in me jealousy from a very young age. It made me feel "less than", like I wasn't good enough. Those were hard feelings to process for such a young tyke. They were real feelings, even if I didn't quite understand them or how they would play into my adult life. One thing those days did for me was create a drive in me to succeed.

When I didn't succeed at things, I would shove my mind into the recesses of self-pity and I was off to the races in my head, not on the playground. I remember a time a Jacob's Well. I had been processing manager one day in September, 2013 and I was elated! I was so excited to be picked first. I was so eager to show others what I could do and I was destined to succeed! But I didn't succeed.

In my eagerness, insecurity, and inherent need for perfection I hurt people. I made them feel less than. I looked down on them as if they didn't know what they were doing. AGAIN. I made a big mess out of something that could have been so easily handled. The next day, I was picked second and my big egotistical balloon of a head got popped right there in front of everyone. I had to quickly revert back to who God said I was in HIM in order to make it through that day. The spirit of Jealousy was on my like a long lost friend and it had the potential to take me out. Along with it tagged

Haughtiness and Pride and they were MORE than willing to pick me first for their team. It's the "I'm the Center of the Universe" mentality and it doesn't work for God. He wants to be the center of MY universe.

Proverbs 16:18 – Pride goes before destruction a haughty spirit before a fall.

I didn't anticipate the stumbling blocks that day. I didn't see myself the way I should. I wasn't going to repent of a sin I didn't even know I had. Ask anyone around me that day and they probably could have told you how aware THEY were of what was really going on.

Romans 12:16 – Live in harmony with one another. Do not be proud, but be willing to associate with people of low position. Do not be conceited.

DANG! It spells it out right there! And I missed it! You have no IDEA the gratitude that I have for being put in second place the next day. If they hadn't been led by the Spirit of God to change the work schedule and get me out of my pride, I would have been as arrogant as Henry VIII who made up his own religion in order to marry some girl. WOW! In all honesty, I didn't like being in second place the next day, but I am always in first place with God and I should put Him first place in my life or the enemy wouldn't mind sending my old friends to trip me up yet again.

John 3:30 – He must increase, but I must decrease.

Matthew 6:33 – But seek first his kingdom and his righteousness, and all these things will be given to you as well.

TWENTY – *Not In Season*

Mark 11:12-14; 20-21 – The next day as they were leaving Bethany, Jesus was hungry. 13 Seeing in the distance a fig tree in leaf, he went to find out if it had any fruit. When he reached it, he found nothing but leaves, because it was not the season for figs. 14 Then he said to the tree, "May no one ever eat fruit from you again." And his disciples heard him say it. 20 In the morning, as they went along, they saw the fig tree withered from the roots. 21 Peter remembered and said to Jesus, "Rabbi, look! The fig tree you cursed has withered!"

It was late September and a day I will never forget. Myself and the other girls at Jacob's Well were on the transport coming home from the store and we started having a long discussion about this fig tree. We mulled it over, turned it upside down and around, probably spoiled the meaning of it all together because we didn't know any better.

Sometimes it's easy to turn scriptures around to make it fit current circumstances and turn it on others. THANKFULLY, God is all knowing and He hears everything.

That very night He sent a beautiful woman of God from another state to our door to give us a devotion. Guess what she talked about? You got it - the fig tree. My whole perspective and outlook on life changed in an instant. Isn't that just like God?

From the scripture, I know that it wasn't the season for figs. Figs bloom in late spring and early fall and this was EARLY spring. The tree itself LOOKED fruitful. It had all the markings of being a good fruit bearing tree but it had no fruit.

I love how in the King James version it says this in verse 14 – 'And Jesus answered and said unto it.' Jesus was passing by and he expected this tree to have fruit because all of its leaves were in. I wonder what the fig tree said to Jesus before He ANSWERED it.

If it was like me, it was giving Him a whole bunch of excuses as to why there was no fruit on its leafy branches. It wasn't in season after all. The tree probably made mention that it the fault of someone or something else (the person who planted it, the weather, the ground it was in, etc) and gave a bunch of "BUTS" and excuses before Jesus ANSWERED the tree and cursed it.

John 15:16 – You did not choose me, but I chose you and appointed you so that you might go and bear fruit – fruit that will last – and so that whatever you ask in my name the Father will give you.

Here is what I am getting at and what that woman drove home that night and even into the next day when she preached our church service - I can look like I bear fruits of the spirit. I can put on a charade like no other because I became very good at doing that for the enemy. I can put out some leaves and make everyone else think I have good fruit (IN or OUT of season). Here is the kicker. JESUS IS ALWAYS PASSING BY.

When my Lord passes by, do I want to just LOOK good or do I want to BE good? In or out of season, I need to continue to bear the fruits of His Spirit because I don't want to be cursed and just wither away. He sees everything. He knows my heart. He knows if I am bearing good fruit or not and He knows before I even have to tell Him. And I want His answer to me to be:

"Well done, good and faithful servant." (Matthew 25:23) Galatians 5:22-23 – But the fruit of the Spirit is love, joy, peace, forbearance, kindness, goodness, faithfulness, 23 gentleness and self-control.

I am expected to bear unexpected fruit in supernatural ways for my Savior because He is IN ME and is my fertilizer, my water, my trunk and strong branches!!

PART TWO

HOME, SWEET HOME

My Walk After Graduation
The Leading Up to the Fall

PART TWO
TABLE OF CONTENTS

21 – God is in Charge

I have been under attack the past 2 days - in my mind, in my heart, physically, emotionally, spiritually. And I know why. It's because I am being obedient. I am making a few sacrifices in the next few weeks and my body is not happy about it. The old me wants to complain and rip a new one into anyone who gets in my way. The new me wants to see the blessings that are just around the corner. satan is trying to stop me from doing what I am doing any way he can so that I don't get closer to God, and so I don't receive my blessings, and so that I don't bless people around me. I need to remember that God is IN CHARGE all the time and He knows what I am going through, what I will continue to go through, and how I will come out on the other side.

I am going to be still through this and remind myself that I don't have anything to complain about. I was reading recently about Abraham and Isaac in Genesis 22. That story took me to an ENTIRELY different level. There are so many different ways of looking at obedience. Sometimes obedience feels like sacrifice, and it is to a degree. But for me obedience may be painful at the moment, but it ALWAYS brings joy, peace, happiness, a feeling of succeeding at something, satisfaction, and rewards!

God called out to Abraham and told him to take his only son, Isaac (the son Abraham had been waiting for for 25 years) up a mountain to offer Isaac as a burnt offering to the Lord. AND HE DID! I can actually picture this. My children are no longer with me (they live in another state). I can feel the range of emotions the man must be feeling; the desire for them to be near, the hurt and the pain of not seeing them or talking to them, the thoughts of "WHY ME" when I am doing everything right. I empathize with Abraham as he carries his son up a mountain. I can feel his pain. He is even comforting his son as they travel to their destination. And THEN....an angel of the Lord comes in to save the day at the very last minute!

Genesis 22:12-18 - "Do not lay a hand on the boy," he said. "Do not do anything to him. Now I know that you fear God, because you have not withheld from me your son, your only son." Abraham looked up and there in a thicket he saw a ram caught by its horns. He went over and took the ram and sacrificed it as a burnt offering instead of his son. So Abraham called that place The Lord Will Provide "Jehovah-Jireh". And to this day it is said, "On the mountain of the Lord it will be provided." The angel of the Lord called to Abraham from heaven a second time and said, "I swear by myself, declares the Lord, that because you have done this and have not withheld your son, your only son, I will surely bless you and make your descendants as numerous as the stars in the sky and as the sand on the seashore. Your descendants will take possession of the cities of their enemies, and through your offspring all nations on earth will be blessed, BECAUSE YOU HAVE OBEYED ME."

I want to be someone who goes beyond the expected. If I give to God what He asks, then He will return to me far more than I could dream! It doesn't matter what I give Him, whether it's caffeine for a few weeks or full control of the circumstances surrounding my children, he just wants me to be obedient!! The biggest part of my Christian walk is going to be in the waiting. But I am willing to wait.

Ephesians 6:12 – For our struggle is not against flesh and blood, but against the rulers, against the authorities, against the powers of this dark world and against the spiritual forces of evil in the heavenly realms. Luke 6:38 – Give and it will be given to you. A good measure, pressed down, shaken together and running over, will be poured into your lap. For with the measure you use, it will be measured to you.

I can put up a fight, or I can trust the Lord. I can offer up a little, or I can offer up a lot. He knows my heart, and He understands my motives. So I will keep pressing on. I will continue to be obedient regardless of the fight around me, and I will praise Him in the storm!! I will not give up 5 minutes before the miracle.

22 — The Waiting Game

There is a lot going on TODAY that brings back memories of just a few months ago and memories of long ago. I am kinda-sorta in the process of looking for a job and we have major transportation issues. We live in the country and share a car and I don't have a license. I have fears, doubts, insecurities and they still pop up from time to time. I am finally starting to feel better from this flu and so I am beginning to catch up on some of the journals that I have been writing from and I was reminded of my state of mind back in early July, 2013. A place in my mind that I don't really want to replay in today's scenario.

I am so grateful for these journals because it reminds me of where I was and the holes I stepped in so that I don't make the same mistake twice. Even though I had just TRULY given myself to the Lord in July, the battle for my soul was still on. satan started attacking my relationship with my husband, my thoughts about my children, and my relationships with people that I worked with everyday at Jacob's Well. I was a HOT MESS. It's hard getting clean alone, but throw in a marriage, a husband that is battling his own demons, a lack of control, a custody situation, child support issues, finances, a messed up living situation, impatience, thinking of myself WAY more highly than I should, FEAR of the unknown, and ALL THAT is a recipe for disaster. All of those things would have sent me back out to my "comfort zone" in the streets if I had an opportunity. That's CRAZY! But it's true.

I was looking over my spiritual journal and I came across some pretty interesting things that were written down at the same time I was battling emotions that I had never before allowed myself to feel.

James 5:7 – Be patient, then, brothers and sisters, until the Lord's coming. See how the farmer waits for the land to yield its valuable crop, patiently waiting for the autumn and spring rains.

If I get what I want immediately, I am a spoiled little kid that isn't growing. I always got what I wanted on the street, which is why it was an easy escape route. Not anymore. Impatience is the fruit of pride. Yuck.

Waiting is a part of life - Waiting for the miracle, waiting for the home, waiting for my license, waiting for a financial break, waiting for a glimmer of hope for reconciliation with my kids, waiting on a job.

Romans 12:3 – For by the grace given me I say to every one of you: Do not think of yourself more highly than you ought, but rather think of yourself with sober judgment, in accordance with the faith God has distributed to each of you.

The proud person (that would be me) thinks so highly of herself that she believes she should never be inconvenienced in any way. Thinking with a SOBER mind, humbly, means I will not display impatience toward God or man.

Colossians 3:12 – Therefore, as God's chosen people, holy and dearly loved, clothe yourselves with compassion, kindness, humility, gentleness and patience.

This scripture reminds me the kind of behavior I should be displaying in EVERY situation. I want to find myself living a quality of life that is not just endured but enjoyed to the fullest. Even while I'm waiting.

1 Peter 5:6 – Humble yourselves, therefore, under God's mighty hand, that he may lift you up in due time.

IN DUE TIME!!! Possibly NOT TODAY.

Proverbs 3:3-5 – Let love and faithfulness never leave you; bind them around your neck, write them on the tablet of your heart. Then you will win favor and a good name in the sight of God and man. Trust in the Lord with all your heart and lean not on your own understanding.

I am not smart enough to run my life on my own. I tried and I failed...miserably. It's time to get comfortable not knowing. It's time I die to my old ways and my own timing and become alive to God's will and way for me. I do not want to be unhappy and unfulfilled because I am too busy trying to make things happen instead of waiting patiently for God. The devil is sneaky. satan knows that the flesh profits nothing.

Romans 13:14 – Rather, clothe yourselves with the Lord Jesus Christ, and do not think about how to gratify the desires of the flesh. Lord, I want Your will in Your timing. I do not want to be ahead of You, nor do I want to be behind You. Help me Father to wait patiently for You and to walk beside You and to trust You.

23 – *The Geographical Cure*

I was a nomad, moving from place to place, always looking for a way out of my mess. It comes natural to me. We moved a LOT when I was a kid. I think I moved at least 20 times by the time I graduated college, and all in the same town. It was after I graduated college that I realized moving away meant running away. That was when I started with the "Geographical Cure".

My mom got into a terrible car accident while I was finishing my senior year in college. It was terrifying. I was ending a bad relationship at the same time, so moving away after graduation was a way to escape. So I did. The military was responsible for some moves, but I always left destruction in my wake. After my divorce, moving was the only option, then after my suicide attempt, another move to another state. I was always moving, always seeking something, always looking for peace; a place where people didn't know me, a place where I could at least try, a new beginning, and always a new failure. IT DOESN'T WORK. Why? Because I always took myself with me.

My free will and choices put me in bad places. God didn't put me there.

Exodus 20:1-4 – I am the Lord your God, who brought you out of Egypt, out of the land of slavery. You shall have no other gods before me. You shall not make for yourself an image in the form of anything in heaven above or on the earth beneath or in the waters below. You shall not bow down to them or worship them; for I, the Lord your God, am a jealous God, punishing the children for the sin of the parents to the third and forth generation of those who hate me, but showing love to a thousand

generations of those who love me and keep my commandments.

Other gods being drugs, alcohol, people, money, work, things, situations - each one representing a different aspect of life. I worshiped them and concentrated on them for personal identity. And I always ended up back in my Egypt, my land of slavery. I got stuck chasing a nightmare because I didn't obey this very simple command to live in the dream.

Isaiah 59:1-2 – Surely the arm of the Lord is not too short to save, nor his ear too dull to hear. But your iniquities have separated you from God; your sins have hidden his face from you, so that he will not hear.

I cut myself off from the one thing that could actually save me. I sat in isolation with my little gods and wondered why in the world I couldn't get it right.

Ephesians 2:1-10 – As for you, you were dead in your transgressions and sins, in which you used to live when you followed the ways of this world and the ruler of the kingdom of the air, the spirit who is now at work in those who are disobedient. All of us also lived among them at one time, gratifying the cravings of our flesh and following its desires and thoughts. Like the rest, we were by nature deserving of wrath. But because of his great love for us, God, who is rich in mercy, made us alive with Christ even when we were dead in transgressions – it is by grace you have been saved. And God raised us up with Christ and seated us with him in the heavenly realms in Christ Jesus, in order that in the coming ages he might show the incomparable riches of his grace, expressed in his kindness to us in Christ Jesus. For it is by grace you have been saved, through faith – and this is not from yourselves, it is the gift of God – not by works, so that no one can boast. For we are God's handiwork, created in Christ Jesus to do good works, which God prepared in advance for us to do.

No longer will I run away, I will run to. I will not ever move again unless GOD tells me to. And I am content in being exactly where I am, because Christ is with me!!

Revelation 12:11 - They triumphed over him by the blood of the Lamb and the word of their testimony; they did not love their lives so much as to shrink from death. Romans 12:1-3-Therefore, I urge you, brothers and sisters, in view of God's mercy, to offer your bodies as a living sacrifice, holy and pleasing to God - this is your true and proper worship. Do not conform to the pattern of this world but be transformed by the renewing of your mind. Then you will be able to test and approve what God's will is- His good, pleasing and perfect will. For by the grace given me I say to every one of you: Do not think of yourself more highly than you ought, but rather think of yourself with sober judgment, in accordance with the faith God has distributed to each of you.

24 – The Ten Commandments

In reading in Exodus about the ten commandments, I was reminded that I used to think they were hogwash. I thought they were for the people of that day, not for me. So I broke every single one of them. If it weren't for the love God has for me and Jesus dying on the cross for me, you can bet on judgment day I would stand before them GUILTY as charged and would be put into a hand basket headed straight for hell. I am a sinner. Through and through. In my study bible, it really lays out the commandments as they were spoken to Moses on Mount Sinai, but also what Jesus had to say about them. So I am going to share how this affects me.

#1 - ***Exodus 20:3 – You shall have no other gods before me.***
Matthew 4:10 – Worship the Lord your God, and serve him only.

I worshiped a lot of gods other than the One True God. I worshiped drugs, money, time, things, people, homes, cars, cell phones....the list goes on and on. It's hard to see it at the time, but anything that comes before the Lord is a mini-god. I have to check myself daily. GUILTY

#2 - ***Exodus 20:4-6 – You shall not make for yourself an image in the form of anything in heaven above or on the earth beneath or in the waters below. 5 You shall not bow down to them or worship them; for I, the Lord your God, and a jealous God, punishing the children for the sin of the parents to the third and fourth generations of those who hate me, 6 but showing love to a thousand generations of those who love me and keep my commandments.***

Luke 16:13 – No one can serve two masters.

This goes with #1. Putting things like money and inanimate objects and people ahead of what God wanted for me. I concentrated too much on "things" for personal identity and meaning. GUILTY.

#3 - *Exodus 20:7 – You shall not misuse the name of the Lord your God, for the Lord will not hold anyone guiltless who misuses his name.*

Matthew 5:34 – But I tell you, do not swear an oath at all; either by heaven, for it is God's throne.

Blasphemy at its finest. Throwing His sacred name around to prove a point. The point is that it made me sound silly and ignorant. GUILTY.

#4 - *Exodus 20:8 - Remember the Sabbath day by keeping it holy.*
Mark 2:27-28 – The Sabbath was made for man, not man for the Sabbath. So the Son of Man is Lord, even on the Sabbath.

I need to spend unhurried time in worship and rest each week. But how many times, even on Sundays, do I forget to take it easy? There is so much rushing around that I forget to take in what is happening around me, that people are being set free, that God is at work in my life and the lives of those within arms reach. God is not in THAT and there is no rest in that either. GUILTY.

#5 - *Exodus 20:12 – Honor your father and mother, so that you may live long in the land the Lord your God is giving you.*

Matthew 10:37 – Anyone who loves their father and mother more than me is not worthy of me.

Whew! Where do I start? I threw off my belief of God after my dad died, so I loved everything and everyone ahead of him. I loved my story about my dad and was addicted to it. I put him over God every day. I also loved my parents, but I did not honor them. I fought them at every turn unless I needed something then I sung their praises. GUILTY.

#6 - *Exodus 20:13 – You shall not murder.*

Matthew 5:22 – Anyone who is angry with a brother or sister will be subject to judgment.

I have never actually killed anyone, but I have killed them in my heart. I refused to forgive, so they were in turn dead to me. GUILTY.

#7 - *Exodus 20:14 – You shall not commit adultery.*

Matthew 5:28 – Anyone who looks at a woman lustfully has already committed adultery with her in his heart.

Yes, I committed adultery. More than once. Am I proud of that? Absolutely not. But it happened. GUILTY.

#8 - *Exodus 20:15 – You shall not steal*

Matthew 5:40 – If anyone wants to sue you and take your shirt, hand over your coat as well.

I have shoplifted, I have stolen from friends, I have stolen from family, I have stolen from strangers. All to support a habit that was slowly killing me physically and emotionally. GUILTY.

#9 - *Exodus 20:16 – You shall not give false testimony against your neighbor.*

Matthew 12:36 – Everyone will have to give account on the day of judgment for every empty word they have spoken.

What I say reveals what is in my heart. And I have lied on people in order to make myself look better. It has also been done to me. I have spoken so negatively over my own life that I believe I spoke some things that happened to me right into existence. Lying to myself, lying to others, falsifying information, this list goes on and on. GUILTY.

#10 - ***Exodus 20:17 – You shall not covet your neighbor's house. You shall not covet your neighbor's wife, or his male or female servant, his ox or donkey, or anything that belongs to your neighbor.***

Luke 12:15 – Be on your guard against all kinds of greed.

JEALOUSY!!! There it is. Wishing and hoping and even praying for the same blessings that I see others have. GUILTY.

NOW FOR THE GOOD NEWS!! Like I said before, I should be going straight to hell. In Moses time, people would have to sacrifice animals and pour their blood on the altar and even on themselves in order to get to God. It symbolized their covenant with the Lord. It also symbolized that one life had been given for another and the penalty for their sin had been paid and they could be reunited with God. Jesus was OUR sacrificial lamb, spotless and without blemish.

Romans 5:6, 8-10 – You see, at just the right time, when we were still powerless, Christ died for the

ungodly. 8 But God demonstrates His own love for us in this: While we were still sinners, Christ died for us. 9 Since we have now been justified by His blood, how much more shall we be saved from God's wrath through Him! 10 For if, while we were God's enemies, we were reconciled to him through the death of His Son, how much more, having been reconciled, shall we be saved through His life!

I was far too weak and rebellious to do anything to get ready for salvation. I wouldn't have known what to do anyway. I was no use to God but He loved me anyway. My life will continue to expand and deepen by means of Jesus' resurrected life!! He hung on the cross and shed His blood so that my sins could be wiped away and I could walk into the throne room, NOT GUILTY!!!!

1 Peter 2:24-25 - "He himself bore our sins" in his body on the cross, so that we might die to sins and live for righteousness; "by his wounds you have been healed." 25 For "you were like sheep going astray," but now you have returned to the Shepherd and Overseer of your souls.

25 – Rebel Without a Cause

I have always had a problem with authority. I looked down on those in authority over me and I always thought I was smarter than them, that I knew best. I had this problem at work, at home, at church, at the drive-in, at restaurants - everywhere I went. Just look where it got me - Alone.

I had to deal with A LOT when it came to my authority issues at Jacob's Well. It was a painful lesson to learn. Even though I knew it was what needed to be done in order to have peace in my life, it was a battle for me nearly every day. I am so grateful to be able to look at my leaders today with respect. I want to honor them, to do what is right, to listen to them. They might have a very good lesson for me and I will miss the blessing if I'm not listening and always putting in my two cents.

**Romans 13:1-5 – Let everyone be subject to the governing authorities, for there is no authority except that which God has established. The authorities that exist have been established by God. 2 Consequently, whoever rebels against the authority is rebelling against what God has instituted, and those who do so will bring judgment on themselves.
3 For rulers hold no terror for those who do right, but for those who do wrong. Do you want to be free from fear of the one in authority? Then do what is right and you will be commended.**

4 For the one in authority is God's servant for your good. But if you do wrong, be afraid, for rulers do not bear the sword for no reason. They are God's servants, agents of wrath to bring punishment on the wrongdoer. 5 Therefore, it is necessary to submit to the authorities, not only because of possible punishment but also as a matter of conscience.

This gives me motivation to pray for my leaders. Then at that time, I become a willing person interceding on their behalf. It causes me to then look at them in a completely different light; to see them as a vessel that the Lord put in my life to teach me how to be a better leader myself. It also helps me better submit to the authority of the Lord, and that is the most important thing for me to do in ANY situation.

Hebrews 13:17 – Have confidence in your leaders and submit to their authority, because they keep watch over you as those who must give an account. Do this so that their work will be a joy, not a burden, for that would be of no benefit to you.

It was always my way or not at all. I went around that circle time and time and time again. The Lord kept bringing the test back and He would sit back and wait for me to give my thoughts to Him so that He could have His way. I love how Susan and Asa always said that when we are being given the lessons, the Teacher is always there.

When it is time for the test, it's like crickets...I hear chirping and nothing else. I had to learn this lesson then put it into practice every single day. Sometimes I got an A, most days I failed miserably. But it's not how I fall, it's how I get back up!! Some days I would knock myself down and have to pull myself up off the floor and try all over again. It's just part of life. God DEMANDS that I give up my own way and be pliable in HIS hands! IT'S NOT ALL ABOUT ME!

Webster defines stubborn as difficult to handle, manage, or treat; unreasonably or perversely unyielding. It defines rebellious as refusing to obey rules or authority or to accept normal standards of behavior, dress, etc.; having or showing a tendency to rebel; resisting treatment or management. Both of those described me. I put that in past tense because it's not who I am anymore thanks to the patient people at Jacob's Well showing me the scriptures to help deal with my persistent disobedience.

1 Samuel 15:22-23 – Does the Lord delight in burnt offerings and sacrifices as much as in obeying the Lord? To obey is better than sacrifice, and to heed is better than the fat of rams. 23 For rebellion is like the sin of divination, and arrogance like the evil of idolatry. Because you have rejected the word of the Lord, he has rejected you as king.

I used to think I was just strong-minded but that is not the case at all. As long as I am rebelling, I am going against all that God has planned for me. If my heart isn't in it, then I am just being hollow and empty. Without true obedience there is no proper respect for the people around me and in turn for the Lord.

Romans 5:19 – For just a through the disobedience of the one mane the many were made sinners, so also through the obedience of the one man the many will be made righteous.

My decisions and my rebellion and my bad attitude affects EVERYONE around me. Jesus was obedient, and now I can trade my sin for His righteousness and stop being such a nuisance to those in authority over me. Joyce Meyer says, "Obedience closes the gates of hell and opens the windows of heaven." AMEN!

Isaiah 55:8-9 – "For my thoughts are not your thoughts, neither are your ways my ways, 9 as the heavens are higher than the earth, so are my ways higher than your ways and my thoughts than your thoughts."

Who am I to think that I have it so much together that I can put down and rebel against everything that comes my way when the Lord is at work it me? His ways and His thoughts should be my ways and my thoughts. I am nothing without Him anyway.

2 Corinthians 10:5-6 – We demolish arguments and every pretension that sets itself up against the knowledge of God, and we take captive every thought to make it obedient to Christ. 6 And we will be ready to punish every act of disobedience once your obedience is complete.

And there is the answer. I fight against my own mind and my own thoughts, when ALL I must do is turn my thoughts over to Jesus and become obedient to His word. It's a struggle for someone who has been rebelling for over 20 years. There is no point in rebellion. NONE. It gets me nowhere. I wish I could say I had this down pat, but it's still a battle for me from time to time. I thank God every day for sending people my way who help me walk away from the plank and back onto to the majestic ship of the Lord!

26 – *Stubbornness*

In looking back at my notes from Jacob's Well, I see quite clearly that God was trying to talk to me then and I believe He is speaking to me now. I am pretty close to finding employment and I feel the Lord is really preparing me for how He wants me to be in the workforce. I jacked all this up so many times at Jacob's Well that this refresher course is just what I need today!

Another benefit of journaling and looking back, not at where I need to go, but how far I have come! You couldn't tell me ANYTHING without me getting my panties in a wad. I would take so much offense at the smallest things then I would immediately get on the defense. Sometimes I needed to hear what was being said to me so I wouldn't repeat the same mistake. I can't hear what is being said when I am unwilling to change.

There I go being stubborn again. Offense is a spiritual hangnail. It just sits there and becomes a nuisance until the offended party decides to see their part and forgive the offender. The best time to forgive someone is the MINUTE they hurt my feelings because offenses are only lies from the enemy to keep me trapped in self-pity.

1 Peter 5:8 – Be alert and of sober mind. Your enemy the devil prowls around like a roaring lion looking for someone to devour.

When I am a lover of people, through Christ, then I will not be so easily offended. I will be able to see them as Christ sees them and be more open to receiving what it is they have to offer me.

Proverbs 4:23 – Above all else, guard your heart, for everything you do flows from it.

Again, I say, out of the heart, the mouth speaks. It's only an offense when I take it that way and when I choose to react to it in a negative way instead of reacting with love and gentleness. If I want to be happy, I should consider trying to make others happy. Offense is unproductive and it is a stumbling stone. It steals everything and produces nothing.

Psalm 119:169 – May my cry come before you, Lord; give me understanding according to your word.

27 – *Grateful for My Life in Christ*

I am so full of gratitude today. I am everyday but today is a little different. Being in addiction was a daily gamble on my life. I knew every single day that I could die. There were times I tried to do it to myself, I had people wanting to kill me, and I nearly died of an overdose right before going to Jacob's Well. I didn't care. That's what drugs did to my spirit. I was dead on the inside, a hollow person with no feelings and no emotion. I was just going through each and every day praying for death to find me quickly.

I found out the day before yesterday that 4 people that I knew died in the town where I used to live in Virginia. All addicts, all suffering their own pain and consequences, lost to the world - and they all killed themselves in the same week. My heart is broken for them, because I KNOW what is on the other side of the pain. So did they. But they chose to turn away from it and I chose to turn to it.

Jesus is the ONLY answer!!! I know their pain. It is very familiar to me, and that kind of sorrow won't go away all by itself. It can't be willed into non-existence, it can't be talked through until my face goes blue, it can't be pushed aside by a drug or drink. It has to be put at the foot of the cross and LEFT THERE. It needs to be LEFT AT THE FEET OF JESUS. He wants my pain. He doesn't want me to suffer and He sure doesn't want me dead. He gave me grace and mercy as a free gift; it was my choice as to accept it or throw it in the trash.

Ecclesiastes 1:18 – For with much wisdom comes much sorrow; the more knowledge, the more grief.

Every time I got clean, I learned more about who I really was. When I would relapse, getting clean again was so hard because of the sorrow I found in wisdom which was knowing what to do and not doing it and then feeling sorry for myself. Evil became more evident and I was evil. That's a hard pill to swallow. For me, all it took to get out of that sad mindset that those people found themselves in was to submit all my despair to Christ.

2 Corinthians 7:10 – Godly sorrow brings repentance that leads to salvation and leaves no regret, but worldly sorrow brings death.

Godly sorrow is being sorry for my sins but changing my behavior and making a choice to become who Christ says I am. Worldly sorrow is feeling sorry for myself because I got caught and that just leads to more self-pity.

Philippians 1:3 – I thank my God every time I remember you.

You know what? I thank my God every time I remember ME. Who I used to be, what I should have been, where I should have been, and where I am today. Today I am walking with Jesus because He saved me. I didn't save myself. Of course, I had to be WILLING to listen to Him and obey Him, but He did the rest. Jesus has the power to save and to transform and I got both! As unworthy and broken as I was, He loved me and gave it to me anyway! That is grace and for that I am grateful! Here is the good news...it is available to EVERY SINGLE PERSON ON EARTH.

1 Corinthians 15:57 – But thanks be to God! He gives us the victory through our Lord Jesus Christ.

Powerful!! Easy!! Full of LOVE!! Full of Compassion!! GRACE AND MERCY!!! My gratitude is pouring forth because I am not who I used to be and I am so grateful that I am not lying in the ground somewhere because of my selfishness. Jesus saves!! He died a miserable and lonely and tragic death so that I could be set free and LIVE and live life to the fullest! Hallelujah!!!

Lord, I thank you for who You are and who I am today. I pray for the families of our friends that have passed. I pray for peace and comfort in this time when questions far outweigh the answers. Bless them Lord with the peace that passes all understanding. I pray for those still out there doing it their way. Lord, reach down from on high and snatch them from the fire. Open their hearts to You, Lord. Open their ears to hear you and their eyes to see the truth. Remind them who they are in YOU!! In Jesus Holy Name, AMEN.

28 – *Forgiving the Mile Markers*

I have had several moments in my life that completely changed the course I was on, good or bad. Susan calls them "Mile Markers", places of decision, big moments in time. Through all of my mile markers (and there are too many to count) I made decisions and I chose blame, fear, hate, resentment. I victimized myself; I became addicted to my story. I chose self-loathing, betrayal, envy, jealousy, malice, discord, depression, isolation, self-pity, shame, guilt, remorse. I got to a point where God no longer existed to me. Along with all of that, I put a lot of effort in pretending that I was someone I wasn't. I wanted to be a good person, I just didn't know how. I forgot who I was and I hated the world.

I was reminded this week, in learning that the girls at Jacob's Well were writing forgiveness letters, that it took a LOT for me to forgive others. It took even more for me to forgive myself. Nothing is more painful, yet freeing at the same time, than sitting down to write a letter to myself and praying for forgiveness from the one who caused the most pain - ME. I caused myself pain because I CHOSE to be all the things listed above. Some of my mile markers were not my doing, most were, but they all had the same result - SELF HATE.

To overcome Mile Markers, I need to see them for what they are. I need to see that I was the one who chose which direction to go in. I looked right, I looked left, and most times I went completely backwards. It's where Satan wants me. Walking around in circles; confused, scared, helpless, and hopeless. But Christ wants so much more. He forgave me the day I asked for it. Christ NEVER resists a repentant sinner.

The main thing I had to do was get REAL HONEST with myself and stop feeding people a bunch of stuff just to get by. When I see myself for what I am, God can work on me. Mandy always said, "In order to be free, I must walk out the Truth."

Joshua 1:9 – Have I not commanded you? Be strong and courageous. Do not be afraid; do not be discouraged, because the Lord your God will be with you wherever you go.

Not whenever He feels like, not only when things are going great, but ALL the time. He is with me even as I stand there pondering the direction I am going to take. He is there, cheering me on and guiding me, even when I go the wrong direction. Even when I think it is hard and I am scared silly...HE IS THERE. He has already been where I am going and He will carry me.

2 Timothy 1:12 – That is why I am suffering as I am. Yet this is no cause for shame, because I know whom I have believed and am convinced that he is able to guard what I have entrusted to Him until that day.

Even though I was at my lowest, God still loved me. I may not have succeeded by the world's standards, but His opinion is the only one that really matters. In order to be successful, I have to do what I have never done. And that is to start going in His direction when I reach a mile marker.

2 Corinthians 7:10 – Godly sorrow brings repentance that leads to salvation and leaves no regret, but worldly sorrow brings death.

Worldly sorrow is just regret. I regretted a lot of things - A LOT. But regret is not God's will. Godly sorrow is

DESIRING to change. Change for the good. Never looking back.

Romans 3:23-24 – for all have sinned and fall short of the glory of God, 24 and all are justified freely by his grace through the redemption that came by Christ Jesus.

Stop the presses! I am a sinner, but I have been given GRACE!! It's new EVERY SINGLE DAY!! This is HUGE! I am justified, so I am found NOT GUILTY by reason of Jesus!! LOVE IT! Here is the deal, God KNOWS my heart. I can talk a good talk and walk a good walk, but what is BEHIND my words and my actions has to be real and honest because HE KNOWS. He will continue to heal me but I have to be willing to let go of sin and stop playing the fool, because God is no fool. NO, INDEED.

1 John 3:19-20 – This is how we know that we belong to the truth and how we set our hearts at rest in his presence. 20 If our hearts condemn us, we know that God is greater than our hearts, and he knows everything.

How do I escape the gnawing accusations of my conscience? By setting my heart on God's love. He gave me the Spirit of Jesus so that I would know right from wrong. My conscience is Christ in ME. My Mile Markers today don't look so scary because I see more clearly. I have finally let go and let God and I have finally forgiven myself. It sure wasn't easy, but absolutely necessary for me to move forward.

1 Timothy 1:15-17 – Here is a trustworthy saying that deserves full acceptance: Christ Jesus came into the world to save sinners – of whom I am the worst. 16 But for that very reason I was shown

mercy so that in me, the worst of sinners, Christ Jesus might display his immense patience as an example for those who would believe in him and receive eternal life. 17 Now to the King eternal, immortal, invisible, the only God, be honor and glory forever and ever. AMEN.

29 – Remembering the Pain

For all the women out there who have children, you know having a baby is tough. It's incredibly painful, it's long and drawn out, it is the most exhausting 9 months we ever go through. Going into labor can last a couple of days then giving birth is the hardest thing a female body can endure. But the second it is over and there is a bundle of squirming joy in your arms, all is forgotten. The thoughts of swollen ankles, weight gain, sleepless nights, incontinence, fear, emotional upheaval, weird cravings; and most importantly, THE PAIN, is lost to the joy.

There is the moment where I thought I was crazy when I was holding my son. I thought to myself that it wasn't that bad and I was ready to do it all over again. It's the same for a lot of people getting clean and finding the Lord. It's easy to forget where I was, where I came from, how bad it hurt, how I almost died; how I lost my family, my children, my home, my things, and my soul to the streets. I CAN'T AFFORD TO FORGET.

I was reminded this week by a long string of unrelated (yet related) events that had me thinking hard about how very grateful I am to the family and staff of Jacob's Well. They put up with so very much; yet, they see women walk away and never turn back to give thanks. The staff of Jacob's Well still gives hope, they give of themselves, they sacrifice their families, they sacrifice their time, and they help people get HEALED. They help birth the baby! They wipe our sweaty brows, they coach us through the pain, they hold our hands through the labor, they are right there in the delivery room!! Yet some women walk away and forget that they left their bundle of joy at the door. This is a very small percentage, but it happens all the time.

Facebook is a horror to look at some days because of the sadness I see in girls I sat right next to. Some end up back in jail, prison, homeless, lost to the world, lost to themselves, and some even in the grave. I'm not judging them; I have no right to. I hurt for them. The pain out here in the real world has been here for me the whole time. It's my choice whether or not to pick it back up and hold onto it. For me it was when the pain far exceeded the pleasure that I had to change for life or lose my life and it took me over 20 years to get to that point.

Luke 17:11-19 – Now on his way to Jerusalem, Jesus traveled along the border between Samaria and Galilee. 12 As he was going into a village, ten men who had leprosy met him. They stood at a distance 13 and called in a loud voice, "Jesus, Master, have pity on us!" 14 When he saw them, he said, "Go, show yourselves to the priests." And as they went, they were cleansed. 15 One of them, when he saw he was healed, came back, praising God in a loud voice. 16 He threw himself at Jesus' feet and thanked him – and he was a Samaritan. 17 Jesus asked, "Were not all ten cleansed? Where are the other nine? 18 Has no one returned to give praise to God except this foreigner? 19 Then he said to him, "Rise and go; your faith has made you well."

There are a couple of points behind this scripture. The one (the only one) who came back was a Samaritan, despised by the Jews, an outcast. I was despised by a lot of people and I was definitely an outcast; but, I was healed anyway. I was released from my pain and my prison and I was given hope.

Lepers had to go before priests to prove that they were cleansed of their disease and Jesus sent them off BEFORE they were cleansed. They went in faith, so He healed them as they walked away. They believed. They took off, pain and all, horrible disease and all, and believed.

The six months I spent at Jacob's Well were a lot like this. I knew I was sick, I knew I was in pain, but I believed that I could be healed, so I did things in faith before I saw the evidence. Here is the sad part...of the ten, only one returned to thank Him. My study bible says this, "It IS possible to receive God's great gifts with an ungrateful spirit." WOW. I am so grateful. I want to grow in God's grace. I want to thank Him even when He doesn't ask for it. I want to learn from the pain and never go back.

Childbirth is a beautiful thing so we choose to do that time and again. God gave us the gift of forgetting so we would continue to be fruitful and multiply. I thank Him for that! Nearly losing my life in the process of "birthing" my pain on the street is a whole other ball game. Yet, He STILL gives me the gift of forgetting. I don't want to forget THAT pain. I will go right back to it, just like I would go right back to childbirth, if I choose to forget.

I pray blessings over every single girl who has made the hardest decision of their life to step foot over the threshold of that beautifully anointed place and that safe haven for greatness. I pray for those out there in pain that they find the strength to make another turn when their mile markers come up.

I pray they go in the direction God chooses for them. And I pray for the girls that are out there doing everything they can to walk their salvation out with fear and trembling. They are all courageous. They are all inspiration. They are all world changers. They are STRONG! Give them ALL guidance and love them as only You know how, Lord. Continue to show them who You are. Amen.

THIRTY – *Rock Bottom*

Gosh, how many times did I actually hit rock bottom? Too many to count. Everyone has a different bottom depending on which pit they fell into and how they got there and what it means for them to be stuck. Me? I jumped into my pits head first, knowing exactly what I would find down there. Sure, I blamed others for pushing me in. In doing so I bought myself some time so I could hang out down there and start decorating my mud walls and making it "home". By the time I felt like I had enough, I would beg someone to pull me out and dust me off only to go jump right back in when it got too hard and the clarity of my mind became clouded with doubt, insecurity, oppression, fear, guilt, shame, remorse, and good ole self-loathing. I should have built a diving board on the side of my pit so at least I could practice my slick beautiful moves and at least TRY to look good jumping into that despair that always waited for me at the bottom. A swan dive is much prettier than a belly flop but both have the same result. They both land me in a strangely uncomfortable place - ROCK BOTTOM.

Here is what I DIDN'T know. There is a trap door in the bottom of the pit put there by the enemy. Before long in the pit, boredom sets in for me and I go on a hunt for new adventure (as if my current adventure wasn't destructive enough). I find the trap door of temptation and hop right in to a much dirtier, much darker place with no comfort at all, no curtains to hang here, no pictures on the wall. It took a lot more effort, but I eventually got out. The next time I jumped in I went straight through THAT door and through another, then another, and ANOTHER. My rock bottom became so low that I couldn't even see a sliver of light. No hope.

Judges 6:6-10 -Midian so impoverished the Israelites that they cried out to the Lord for help. 7 When the Israelites cried out to the Lord because of Midian, 8 he sent them a prophet, who said, "This is what the Lord, the God of Israel says: I brought you out of Egypt, out of the land of slavery. 9 I rescued you from the hand of the Egyptians. And I delivered you from the hand of all your oppressors; I drove them out before you and gave you their land. 10 I said to you, 'I am the Lord your God; do not worship the gods of the Amorites, in whose land you live.' But you have not listened to me."

Take responsibility for my own actions? That was a new concept. God has always gone before me. He has never left me. Even when I was lost to sin and a foot soldier for the enemy, God was with me. I CHOSE to jump into my pits. I CHOSE to disobey and then call out to God from rock bottom. I did that AFTER I jumped in and not before. One of the greatest lessons I have learned in all of this is to reach out BEFORE taking my Olympic game worthy leap into the pit.

Genesis 26:25 – Isaac built an altar there and called on the name of the Lord. There he pitched his tent, and there his servants dug a well.

Dig your well, nourish yourself for once from the living water God gave you. Pitch your tent and CALL ON GOD!! Don't jump in. It's a wet, cold, dark, musty place and it isn't your home. Obey God no matter what everyone else is doing or saying. His voice and opinion is the only One that matters!

Zechariah 13:9b – They will call on my name and I will answer them; I will say, "They are my people," and they will say, "The Lord is our God."

31 – *Lousy Jealousy*

Oh Jealousy! In the words of author, Margaret Atwood: "You can only be jealous of someone who has something you think you ought to have yourself." Jealousy is a misconception of the truth. It makes me lose my perspective of the truth and love of God. I then in turn lose trust in His ability to do what is best in any circumstance I find myself in. I would love to say that I'm not a jealous person. I used to be jealous of everyone and everything, always trying to "live up to the Jones'". Today, not so much, but I AM suffering in silence at this very moment.

I'm just going to get honest here because when I speak the lies of the enemy out loud, the coward loses his power over me. I'm going to shatter this stronghold right here and right now because I don't want to feel this way and quite frankly it makes me sick. I am jealous of other women that have also graduated Jacob's Well that are already in the process of getting their children back. I'm also angry at those who choose not to be around their children full time because I would give anything to be in a position to even see mine on a regular basis (or just once for that matter). So now, not only am I jealous, but I am judging.

Whew - there it is - out there for the world to see. Now it's time to replace the lie with God's TRUTH and get this up off me. I first want to say that being jealous and judgmental is not in my heart and I am over the moon happy for these beautiful, strong, courageous women of God. God is moving in their lives and what a blessing! It gives me all the more reason to stomp this lie back into hell where it belongs.

James 4:2 – You desire but do not have, so you kill. You covet but you cannot get what you want, so you quarrel and fight. You do not have because you do not ask God.

That truth HURTS. I do ask God for what my desires are with my children and for some reason I keep taking back His power over my situation and I try to figure out ways to make it happen in my own strength. Then begins the quarrel within myself and I begin to start looking at everyone else and not myself. I forget about all the things that are going great in my life and all the blessings God is bestowing on me at breakneck speeds. I take back what I originally surrendered. And it is EXHAUSTING. My motives are not completely pure. Plain and simple. That is a hard truth.

Colossians 1:9-14 – For this reason, since the day we heard about you, we have not stopped praying for you. We continually ask God to fill you with the knowledge of his will through all the wisdom and understanding that the Spirit gives, 10 so that you may live a life worthy of the Lord and please him in every way: bearing fruit in every good work, growing in the knowledge of God, 11 being strengthened with all power according to his glorious mights so that you may have great endurance and patience, 12 and giving joyful thanks to the Father, who has qualified you to share in the inheritance of his holy people in the kingdom of light. 13 For he has rescued us from the dominion of darkness and brought us into the kingdom of the Son he loves, 14 in whom we have redemption, the forgiveness of sins.

And there it is. I am in a holding pattern so that God can continue to work on my character and I can continue to grow in Him so that I know that every good work comes from HIM ALONE and not in my own strength. Susan Brogan from Jacob's Well said it so clearly yesterday that I nearly fell off my bed reading it. She said, "Logic never undresses in front of pain. Sometimes God digs ditches in our valleys, so bad has got to get worse because bad was just not deep enough and it was not anything you did wrong. Sometimes things need to look utterly impossible so that God can say, 'I couldn't do it until I knew that you saw no way on earth it could be done.' I trust the promise but I have to survive the process." My process is not the same as Suzie Q or Janey L. I am Julie and God is in CONTROL of MY PAIN and MY PROCESS just like He is in control of THEIR PAIN and THEIR PROCESS. I do not want my identity as a Christian woman to be put in jeopardy because I am in the mindset of wanting what others have. Jesus gave me LIFE and FREEDOM!!! He wakes me up every morning with new mercies! When I desire something more than my relationship with God, I am saying that "it" is more important that HIM. OUCH.

Romans 13:9 – The commandments, "You shall not commit adultery," "You shall not murder," "You shall not steal," "You shall not covet," and whatever other command there may be, are summed up in this one command: "Love your neighbor as yourself."

Guess what? I am stealing joy when I covet, I am murdering someone's character when I judge them, and I am SINNING. My new attitude??

1 Corinthians 1:4 – I always thank my God for you and for the gracious gifts He has given you.

32 – *I Surrender ALL*

What is my destiny? I can tell you this much. My destiny was NOT to walk the streets looking for drugs. My destiny was NOT to die lonely and miserable and afraid. My destiny was NOT to live institutionalized. Pastor Tilghman said recently that unless there is a contest, there cannot be a conquest. There have never been truer words spoken. The majority of my adult life was a contest. I was constantly battling against unseen forces that wanted me dead.

Romans 8:29-30 – For those God foreknew he also predestined to be conformed to the image of his Son, that he might be the firtborn among many brothers and sisters. 30 And those he predestined, he also called; those he called, he also justified; those he justified, he also glorified.

God had a goal for me and that was for me to be like Christ. Before I was ever born, He set out my destiny. God has a purpose for me that is not an afterthought. To know that He set me apart before the creation of the world that I live on is some POWERFUL stuff! I can't imagine His heartbreak when I turned from Him time and again to seek my selfish desires when HE KNEW exactly where I was SUPPOSED to be. He is the same yesterday, today, and forever so who needs to change in order to be more like Him? ME. My destiny is to walk out my salvation with fear and trembling and seek the face of God around every single corner. You know what God said to me the other day? I was complaining to Him about how tired I was and how it was too hard now to get up early and have my quiet time. I was making excuses and I was bargaining with GOD about when I could get around to doing the things I had promised Him. Come on now. He said to me, "Child, when you were at Jacob's Well, you were up every single morning at 4:30 for quiet time with me. You then had breakfast and devotion then went to work (and hard work at that) for a good 8 hours. You had devotions at night, you took a shower, you ate, you got ready for bed, and you even had time to socialize with the other girls. Before you went to bed, we shared intimate moments in quiet solitude. Why can't you make time for me today?"

Acts 17:27 – God did this so that they would seek him and perhaps reach out for him and find him, though he is not far from any one of us.

My destiny is to live for Him. I don't want to be standing at gates of heaven after all I have been through only to have Him turn me away as if He didn't know me.

Matthew 7:21-23 - "Not everyone who says to me, 'Lord, Lord,' will enter the kingdom of heaven, but only the one who does the will of my Father who is in heaven."

My destiny was written before I was born and it's up to me to make the right choices to live it out. His Word and His plan for my life will not return void as long as I do what He asks of me.

Isaiah 55:11 – so it is my word that goes out from my mouth: It will not return to me empty, but will accomplish what I desire and achieve the purpose for which I sent it.

33 – *Broken Telephone*

Do you remember the game we played as kids where the teacher would whisper a secret to a child, then have the child tell it to the next child in a whisper, and the news would travel down the line to the last child? Do you also remember that it NEVER made it down the line in its original context? As a kid, I always thought that was so funny. I would laugh uncontrollably as the whisper came to me and I passed it along to someone else. When the teacher would tell us what she had originally said, you would find me on the floor in a fit of giggles. This game isn't so funny as an adult. HELLO!?!?!?!!?! We are adults, right? We deal with adults....RIGHT?!?! Why does this VERY SAME THING still happen today? Is it because of something we are not doing right?

Sometimes the first place to look is into my own heart to find truth in situations that baffle me. Maybe I don't have enough compassion. Maybe I don't have enough sympathy for where people are at any given moment that would lead them to act like 5 year old kids on the playground. Maybe I am too harsh - Maybe, maybe, maybe. Here is what God says:

> **2 Corinthians 4:17-18 – For our light and momentary troubles are achieving for us an eternal glory that far outweighs them all. 18 So we fix our eyes not on what is seen, but on what is unseen, since what is seen is temporary, but what is unseen is eternal.**

There is a greater purpose to our suffering. Our momentary troubles are not here to diminish our faith or make us delusional. When I am feeling shut out or isolated, God is really at work then and NOTHING can separate me from His love.

Ephesians 4:2-3 – Be completely humble and gentle; be patient, bearing with one another in love. 3 Make every effort to keep the unity of the Spirit through the bond of peace. James 1:2-4 – Consider it pure joy, my brothers and sisters, whenever you face trials of many kinds, 3 because you know that the testing of your faith produces perseverance. 4 Let perseverance finish its work so that you may be mature and complete, not lacking anything.

I have a choice. I can sit by and blame everyone else around me for my pain and suffering, or I can see my part and CHOOSE JOY and I can praise God through the storm. Every situation is a chance for me to grow in Christ and to become more like Him. What is the lesson from my Teacher today?

"Be humble, be patient, the battle is already won and you are fighting FROM victory. Have joy, be kind, be compassionate. Think of where others are in their walk and pray for those who persecute you. Lift up My Name. Allow your trials and troubles to draw closer to me. Move from problem to prayer and allow Me to move on your behalf."

This is a secret that I will not keep to myself and I sure won't allow it to pass down the line in a confusing mess! The person at the end of this will know the TRUTH!

34 – *The Green Light*

I am standing at a crossroads. A BIG decision is on the horizon. It requires that I step out of my comfort zone and onto the battle of uncertainty. Do I know what I am up against? Absolutely. Am I scared? Somewhat. Do I trust God even if a few doors get shut along the way? NO DOUBT! Am I alone? NEVER. Has God already gone ahead of me and prepared the way? YES!!! Am I going to win this fight? GOD IS GOING TO WIN! The battle has already been won!

Of course the enemy sneaks in and tries to whisper in my ear that it is too soon, that I'm not in the will of God, that I'm off the my own again and I am going to fail...AGAIN. Is that fear from God? NO.

Exodus 14:13-15 – Moses answered the people, "Do not be afraid. Stand firm and you will see the deliverance the Lord will bring you today. The Egyptians you see today you will never see again. 14 The Lord will fight for you; you need only to be still." 15 Then the Lord said to Moses, "Why are you crying out to me? Tell the Israelites to move on."

God fighting on my behalf doesn't mean I need to be lazy and sit idly by. I have to take a step in the right direction. It means for me that I have to do everything I can, then STAND FIRM. I still have to do my part.

Ephesians 6:13 – Therefore put on the full armor of God, so that when the day of evil comes, you may be able to stand your ground, and after you have done everything, to stand.

God spoke directly to me and told me to move so that He could begin to bless my efforts. I already believe His promises. I feel like David when he was called to the valley to bring provisions to his brothers. He was not prepared to cut off the head of a giant and I feel like I am not either. God was glorified when He alone paved the way and the giant fell to the ground. Sometimes God can't get all the glory when we feel like we do everything in our own strength. Therein lies the hindsight. I see my old mistakes so clearly and today I am going to learn from them. I CANNOT do this alone. Sometimes I have to do things afraid just like Peter did when he stepped out of the boat and joined my Savior on the water.

Matthew 14:28-29 - "Lord, if it's you," Peter replied, "tell me to come to you on the water." 29 "Come," he said. The Peter got down out of the boat, walked on the water and came toward Jesus.

I'm sure his blood was pumping like mine is now. I'm sure he felt a level of excitement like no other time in his life when he KNEW that ALL things are possible with Christ Jesus. My God is bigger than the waves around me, He is greater than the giant in my path, and He fights or me and I fight FROM victory! I'm getting my fight back and Jesus is my Commander in Chief. The green light is flashing GO!!!!

Psalm 23 – The Lord is my shepherd, I lack nothing. 2 He makes me lie down in green pastures, he leads me beside quiet waters, 3 he refreshes my soul. He guides me along the right paths for his name's sake. 4 Even though I walk through the darkest valley, I will fear no evil, for you are with me; your rod and your staff, they comfort me. 5 You prepare a table before me in the presence of my enemies. You anoint my head with oil; my cup overflows. 6 Surely your goodness and love will follow me all the days of my life, and I will dwell in the house of the Lord forever.

35 – *The Blame Thrower*

Have you ever pulled out the blame-thrower, aimed it at whoever was nearby, then ducked for cover? I'm GUILTY. The reality is that some people place unwarranted blame and don't even duck. Ducking for cover would mean they were convicted of the fact that just threw someone under the bus for no reason.

I still have to be very careful because it became a part of who I was and I do not want to drag myself back into THAT pit. When we don't want to shed the light of Truth on our circumstance, falling into the blame-thrower mentality seems like the easiest route. There was a time when I did not want to take responsibility for anything.

The most powerful thing I have ever done in my life is to ask God to show me the truth about myself. When He did, I wanted to run and hide under a bed. I didn't want to face it. The truth about me hurts, but blaming others and throwing them under the bus only to run over them time and again hurts even worse. I took comfort in the fact there are many, many, many examples of people in the Bible using their blame-thrower. I even used those stories as an excuse to keep it up. But they are in the Bible, their nakedness is revealed, and God showed them to me so that I don't make the same mistakes.

The most famous "blame-thrower" incident in the Bible is in Genesis, when Adam and Eve are caught red-handed eating the forbidden fruit.

Genesis 3:12-13 – The man said, "The woman who you put here with me – she gave me some fruit from the tree, and I ate it. Then the Lord God said to the woman, "What is this you have done?" The woman said, "The serpent deceived me, and I ate."

It's always someone else's fault, right??? NOT. I have a choice to make. My life is so much easier when I take responsibility for my own actions. The ones I love are sick and tired of me firing my gun. All it is is a way to shift the guilt, complaining about the adverse circumstances without looking in the mirror. This does not solve any problems, it only serves as an excuse to not change the attitude and behaviors that got me into whatever uncomfortable situation I found myself in.

James 1:13-15 (NIV) – When tempted, no one should day, "God is tempting me." For God cannot be tempted by evil, nor does He tempt anyone, 14 but each person is tempted when they are dragged away by their own evil desire and enticed. 15 Then, after desire has conceived, it gives birth to sin; and sin, when it is full-grown gives birth to death.

Wow, that is a warning like no other. I am responsible for the wrongs I suffer. Everything is a choice. There are always things out of our control, but a decision must be made as how to handle situations. If I choose to stay the victim, everyone else gets the blame, and God is left out of the picture completely. It's the beginning of a death spiral. satan wants us stuck there, blame-thrower in hand and hiding behind a bush because he knows if we face the truth about ourselves and how God sees us, the truth will set us free.

I don't want to be stuck anymore in that cycle of despair. I want the TRUTH! Even if it's painful at the moment, JOY always comes in the morning!!! I need to keep my eyes on God and not the problem! Aren't you tired of making excuses for wrong actions?

John 8:32 – Then you will know the truth, and the truth will set you free!!

Allow the light to meet the dark and let healing begin.

36 – *Like a Flood*

It's Wednesday late afternoon. We are driving in the car on the way back to Hattiesburg after seeing our friends, Tracy and Greg, and their sweet angel, Willow, at the Children's Hospital in Jackson, MS. Now is a time for reflection. I was scared to go. I knew I needed to go support my friends, but I was not looking forward to the memories that I had stored in my heart.

I sat in that Pediatric Intensive Care Unit in the all too familiar surroundings. There was the beeping of the monitors, the hushed talk of the doctors and nurses, the smell of sterilization, the tired looks in the eyes of exhausted parents; yet, the glimmer of hope still shined in the eyes of my friends. I watched as my dear friend consoled her child who was about to undergo yet another blood transfusion, who hadn't eaten in days except through an I.V., fever wracking her poor small body, fussing with a pacifier that offered no satisfaction. I saw myself not so long ago. The memories came in like a flood and nearly swept over my whole being.

Isaiah 44:24 – This is what the Lord says – your Redeemer, who formed you in the womb: I am the Lord, the Maker of all things, who stretches out the heavens, who spreads out the earth by myself.

My children were sick babies. My first lost over 2 pounds in less than 6 weeks following his birth. His skin was ashy, his eyes sunk in, and his skin fell off his bones. He could not keep food down and the doctors couldn't tell me why. We tried everything. My husband (at the time) and I were like ships passing in the night just trying to get through each day. One of us stayed awake around the clock because we weren't sure our son would survive the nights until morning. Each day was a battle and we became scientists in trying to figure out the right combination of formula, milk, water, and cereal that would keep our child from death's door . After walking the halls of a hospital time and time again with a child that was starving to death only to be told by the doctor that he was "failure to thrive" – well - I checked out. I took a mental hiatus and knocked myself out of commission physically, emotionally, and most of all, spiritually. I reverted to the deep parts of my mind and sank into a depression that kept my heart from exploding out of my chest. Once they finally admitted him to the hospital, I was a sad representation of "holding it together".

He had surgery on his Pyloric Sphincter and came through with flying colors. He hasn't had a problem since. My second son then had the same problem, same surgery, faster result. It was when he had to undergo massive skull surgery at the age of 6 months that I got lost again. By the time the huge bed came rolling by with my tiny little baby and 10-15 doctors and nurses tending to him I was back in my cocoon, surrounded by fibers of fear, sadness, inadequacy, hopelessness, and exhaustion that kept my mind and my heart from the pain. I was there for them but I wasn't THERE.

Three surgeries, two babies, a lifetime of regret. But it's not about me. It never has been and never will be. How can what I went through ever help anyone else? When I show the love of Christ and let go. The Lord showed me today, as I was sitting there watching my friend rock her child through a web of tubes and wires, that I am THERE today. I am there spiritually, emotionally, and physically. It is never too late to forgive myself and holding onto those memories as if they define who I am as a person does nothing for anyone. He also showed me that I WAS there for my children, I just didn't want to see it at the time. I wanted to use it as another excuse to jump back into my comfortable pit.

Psalm 8:2 – Through the praise of children and infants you have established a stronghold against your enemies, to silence the foe and the avenger.

I learned a LOT about myself today. I learned that with the help of Jesus, I can overcome my fears and step into a frightening place with terrifying memories and survive. I can be there for someone else and even without saying a word, just BE. I was a good mom going through some horrible moments and I am SO grateful God kept my children alive even when I didn't believe in Him. I am grateful to have been there with my friend today. I am grateful to have seen her faith so strong and to learn from her. What an HONOR.

Mark 10:13-16 – People were bringing little children to Jesus for him to place his hands on them, but the disciples rebuked them. 14 When Jesus saw this, he was indignant. He said to them, "Let the little children come to me, and do not hinder them, for the kingdom of God belongs to such as these. 15 Truly I tell you, anyone who will not receive the kingdom of God like a little child will never enter it." 16 And he took the children in his arms, placed his hands on them and blessed them.

37 – *Stuck in the Busy*

There are some days I get stuck in the busy. I get lost in the shuffle of everyday. I lose sight of the importance of true living and I focus on the world. I get bogged down with the "to-do" list and forget to pray over it. I push myself to limits that I shouldn't and I pay too much attention to the mundane. That is a seriously dangerous place for me. Today is one of those days. I feel like there aren't enough hours. There isn't enough money. There isn't enough prayer, enough hope, enough joy. satan uses this to his advantage and if I'm not careful, depression soon follows.

Psalm 46:10 – He says, "Be still, and know that I am God."

Be still. That is a hard task for this girl. I was so used to moving so quickly so I wouldn't have time for my thoughts that being still for me is almost like punishment in a sad way. Staying busy kept me out of my head. But it is all that is required...just to be still. The "to-do" list is of MY making; it's not of God.

For an addict, being stuck in the busy can be a jumping off point back into the isolation of the disease. Isolation is the key to end the never-ending chatter in the loneliness of the "too-busy" mind. You might ask, "How can being busy and doing things for others and having work and things to do at home be lonely?" It is. It can be. But it doesn't have to be. (Hey...this is deep stuff. It makes sense to me!)

When I am in the loneliness of the "too-busy" mind, in sneaks my old friends - self-doubt, confusion, worry, fear, and paranoia. My mind becomes a little playground. These guys are on the jungle gym and having the best time swinging from the circles being spun in my head. The lies are that my past will always be my present.

My husband who is out camping having a good time in a large group of people will have too much fun without me and will be hanging around women that I don't trust. The people at work are all against me. I should just give up and not do anything anymore. I'm not wanted anywhere I go. LIES, LIES, LIES.

My thoughts when alone and in isolation get me nowhere unless I take them captive and put them at the foot of the cross.

2 Corinthians 10:5 - We demolish arguments and every pretension that sets itself up against the knowledge of God, and we take captive every thought to make it obedient to Christ.

EVERY THOUGHT! If I allow myself this alone time to focus on the "What-If's" and get stuck in the busy, I will forget the purpose set before me and I will choose to look solely to my past for answers. I WILL GO INSANE and look for solitude in dark places. If I choose (AGAIN...It's all about my choices) to focus on the fact that I am NEVER alone, my past does not define my present, Jesus LOVES me, I stand on a solid rock, fear is not of the Lord, and God works everything out for those who love Him; then paranoia, fear, and depression must FLEE at the name of Jesus. I CHOOSE TO BELIEVE THE TRUTH.

Philippians 4:7 - And the peace of God, which transcends all understanding, will guard your hearts and your minds in Christ Jesus.

BE STILL.

38 – The Juggling Act

I am not in the circus. I do not know how to juggle. So why do I always feel like there are so many balls in the air? I have watched people juggle before and it's a hard task. I sure don't know how to do it. I can't even juggle two balls, much less three or four. Sometimes the balls collide with the others and fall to the ground one by one. Sometimes it is perfection, each ball soaring through the air and to heights unexplainable, each one whizzing past the other in arcs of beauty. When God is in charge, the balls are seamlessly speeding through space, never coming in contact with another object until they all fall into a perfect heap into His hands before He makes His bow as the curtain closes. When I am in charge, I end up getting hit in the head by the hard stones as they fail to find their way on their path and just fall completely out of the sky in a confusing and jumbled mess. The curtain closes on me as I am still trying to pick up the pieces of my act, embarrassed and ashamed that I even tried.

Today I feel like I am standing at a crossroads with so many avenues and choices to make that I am crippled with fear. My balls are all in the air and I don't know who is in charge. Do we look for a two bedroom house now as our lease is coming up or wait until the Lord blesses us with children in our home? Do we start looking for a car for me now? How much money are we going to be out if we do both? What will our finances look like 6 months from now if we make these decisions in the next two months? Are we going to be able to have the funds to give back to the ministries that helped us get free? What about the legal stuff I have coming up? Is that going to cost an arm and a leg? What if we get in over our heads? What if we make the wrong decisions? How do we know if we are still in the will of God? On top

Psalm 73:23-26 – Yet I am always with you; you hold me by my right hand. 24 You guide me with your counsel, and afterward you will take me into glory. 25 Whom have I in heaven but you? And earth has nothing I desire besides you. 26 My flesh and my heart may fail, but God is the strength of my heart and my portion forever.

I am going to take this ONE DAY AT A TIME. I am being renewed day by day. I can't be weighed down by past failures because that is what is keeping me in fear. Susan Brogan says all the time that Courage is Fear, one minute later. ONE MINUTE. I don't have to make all these decisions today. The balls are in the air but God has them in the palm of His hand. I am acutely aware of my own insufficiency, so I will REJOICE for I do not do this alone. I am utterly dependent on my Savior to make these decisions for me.

Matthew 5:3 – Blessed are the poor in spirit, for theirs is the kingdom of heaven.

I may be poor in spirit, but I know where my help comes from. I may have a lot of decisions on the horizon, but I know the right s will be opened and the wrong ones shut. The curtain on this chapter is about to close and a new and exciting future is ahead. I won't be picking balls up off the ground this time. Jesus will be standing beside me as we take our bows TOGETHER.

2 Corinthians 6:4-10 – Rather, as servants of God we commend ourselves in every way: in great endurance; in troubles, hardships and distresses; 5 in beatings, imprisonments and riots; in hard work, sleepless nights and hunger; 6 in purity, understanding patience and kindness; in the Holy Spirit and in sincere love; 7 in truthful speech, and in the power of God; with weapons of righteousness and in the right hand and in the left; 8 through glory and dishonor, bad report and good report; genuine, yet regarded as imposters; 9 known, yet regarded as unknown; dying, and yet we live on; beaten, and yet not killed; 10 sorrowful, yet always rejoicing; poor, yet making many rich; having nothing, and yet possessing everything.

39 – *Jesus Prayed*

It's Sunday, April 27th, 2014 and today is my son's birthday. I miss him more than anything.

I am sitting at the table at Jacob's Well, visiting for a few days, enveloped in peace. This place is guarded by angels. I can sense the Holy Spirit hovering over this anointed home as I write. This place is for the broken hearted. It is for the lost. It is for the hopeless, the helpless, the distraught, and the lonely.

I will never forget walking over the threshold here for the first time with so much doubt and insecurity and emptiness that I couldn't even breathe. I love everything about this place; the rose bush that had been cut back while I was here that is now in full bloom, the beautiful green grass in the pastures as far as the eye can see, the trees that lead into the wooded area that provide shelter for the birds and animals, the pond that is home to the symphony of music coming from creatures that seem to keep in time and beat to the music of God's orchestra. I see hope here. I see life. I see potential. I see GLORY!!!

I also see doubt, fear, confusion, worry, anxiety, and sadness on the faces of some of the newer women who have just come from the hell of their own making. And my heart is breaking. God wants us to come to Him, ready and expecting to receive. Regardless of how difficult and draining life can be, He wants us to come to Him because His Power flows freely to those in need.

I read a verse this morning that had me wanting to stand up and shout "HALLELUJAH" into the quiet of the dawn!

John 17:20-23 - "My prayer is not for them alone. I pray also for those who will believe in me through their message, 21 that all of them may be one, Father, just as you are in me and I am in you. May they also be in us so that the world may believe that you have sent me. 22 I have given them the glory that you gave me, that they may be one as we are one – 23 I in them and you in me – so that they may be brought to complete unity. Then the world will know that you sent me and have loved them even as you have loved me."

Jesus prayed for ALL who would follow him, including me and you and the women of Jacob's Well. As I look around the room at the strongest, bravest women I have ever met who are just waking up to get their coffee and have their quiet time with Jesus, hair all a mess, pajamas still on, sleep still in their eyes and dreams still on their minds, I am reminded that I have a purpose in life and that is to share the Good News of what Christ alone can do. I was so lost to the world, yet Jesus still prayed for ME. He prayed that I have unity with people just like me and become unified as powerful witnesses to the reality of God's amazing LOVE!

Hope helps me to see, through the eyes of my heart, things that are not yet. Some of these women don't yet have a clue the GLORY that comes from being unified with Christ. And I pray that they seek with all their heart their destiny, which is to follow God into the hopes and dreams that are in line with His will, in eager anticipation!!

Hebrews 11:1 – Now faith is confidence is what we hope for and assurance about what we do not see.

FORTY – *Friend for Life*

I am at a point in transcribing my journal notes and other notes from Jacob's Well that was a bit of a dark time for me. It was a time when Jesus had to really step in and deal with me in a mighty way regarding certain aspects of my life. It took me a long time to realize that drugs and alcohol were not my problem. I had a relationship problem - With everyone. I was deep in "approval addiction" and didn't even recognize it. I did whatever I needed to do to get on everyone's nice list (whether it be the junkie on the street, the drug dealer, friends on the outside, friends on the inside, or women at Jacob's Well) and all it got me was a ton of grief. I ended up pushing everyone away, even after the drugs were no longer a problem.

I was desperate for love, the kind of love that couldn't come from any human being, yet I was seeking worldly love anyway. I just wanted friendship. I wanted to be friends with the people that were talking about me behind my back right in front of my face. I wanted to befriend those whose hearts were set on their own agendas. I wanted to be friends with those who would gladly stab me in the back, throw me under the bus, and then speak kindness to my face. I was desperate!!

Many a tear were cried and for what?!?! So that I could be distracted by the lies of the enemy and not focus on the truth. Days upon days of journal notes proving that I was drowning in my self-pity and clawing for some sort of surface where I felt I could stand up again and reclaim my "friends" and in all reality reaching for people that I had no right to reach out to.

Therein lies the error of my ways. Jesus is my only friend for life.

Proverbs 13:20 - Whoever walks with the wise becomes wise, but the companion of fools will suffer harm.

Proverbs 22:24-25 - Make no friendship with a man given to anger, nor go with a wrathful man, lest you learn his ways and entangle yourself in a snare.

Well, there you have it. I am to be cautious in my choice of companionship. It took a long time for me to be ok being alone. I had to desire Christ before anything and anyone and when I did, He added unto me some pretty amazing people who are all in it for the right reasons and that is to glorify HIM in everything they do!

Ephesians 4:29-32 - Let no corrupting talk come out of your mouths, but only such as is good for building up, as fits the occasion, that it may give grace to those who hear. And do not grieve the Holy Spirit of God, by whom you were sealed for the day of redemption. Let all bitterness and wrath and anger and clamor and slander be put away from you, along with all malice. Be kind to one another, tender hearted, forgiving one another, as God in Christ forgave you.

I am so grateful for the precious, godly friends that God has placed in my life for such a time as this to show me how to love like Christ first loved me!

41 – *Rejection and Loneliness*

I am feeling a bit deflated here recently (actually this took place last weekend). I don't like rejection at all. It makes me feel like there is something really wrong with me. I have been trying to reach out to people that I graduated Jacob's Well with and to no avail. I am actually beginning to feel a bit stalker-ish so I am packing up my ideas of friendship with these people for awhile. I just want so badly for them to know that they are loved by someone. I know their thoughts, because I have thought them. I know their pain, because I have felt it. I know their loneliness in their isolation, because I too have been there. I just want to help but I feel like all I am doing is spinning my wheels.

Susan used to say that we walked into the program alone and we will walk out alone, but I never wanted to believe that. I wanted to believe that people stayed on the right track. I believed in the fairy tale!! Life isn't like that. It shows up differently for people in unexpected ways and I forget that so easily. Maybe it's because I am lonely. Maybe it's because as much as I enjoy hanging out with my husband every night eating dinner and watching movies, sometimes I just desire to be around girlfriends who get me. Now, my insecurities are starting to pop up all over again and that is breeding ground for Satan to come in with his minions and try to keep me company. NOT GOOD.

Here is the deal...TODAY I AM OK BEING FRIENDS WITH GOD. He will NEVER reject me or leave me and I am NEVER alone! God has a plan for my life and I need to accept the fact that it may very well not include the people who I am trying so desperately to be around. I need good character and maturity and if I am going to gain that by sitting on my couch typing all by myself on my days off, then so be it.

2 Corinthians 5:17 – Therefore, if anyone is in Christ, the new creation has come: The old has gone, the new is here!

I have been recreated. I am beginning a new life under new Leadership. I have been changed from within so my life needs to reflect my new body, my new mind, and my new perspective. This means that I can't let the spirit of Rejection back in because right behind him is Paranoia and y'all REALLY don't want me hanging out with those two, especially together.   I am reminded in my spirit that Jesus was rejected ALL THE TIME.

Philippians 3:10 – I want to know Christ – yes, to know the power of his resurrection and participation in his sufferings, becoming like him in his death.

I want to know Jesus, so to know Him is to suffer like Him. Bring it on!! If it makes me more like my Creator and Savior to go through this and come out refined on the other side, so be it!

Romans 8:17-18 – Now if we are children, then we are heirs – heirs of god and co-heirs with Christ, if indeed we share in his sufferings in order that we may also hare in his glory. 18 I consider that our present sufferings are not worth comparing with the glory that will be revealed in us.

42 – *The Belly of the Whale*

JUNE 17th – 2014 – The Day Before My Relapse – I witnessed firsthand recently someone who ran away from God's leading and I was instantly reminded of the story of Jonah.

Jonah was asked by God to share the good new to the horrible people of Ninevah so they could repent and turn from their evil ways. Jonah ran away and boarded a ship headed the other direction. That is exactly what just happened. God laid a golden opportunity at the feet of my love and asked him to be a prophet to the nation, including close people in his circle, and he ran away in the opposite direction. Jonah ended up being thrown off a ship, caught up in the belly of a whale, and put back on track even against his own will. Once he delivered God's message and followed His leading, Ninevah was saved from death and Jonah became angry and threw a tantrum.

Excuses are nails that build a house of failure. I love how God meets Jonah where he is but doesn't give him a whole lot of relief. We can't run from God. He loves us too much. He has a purpose for us, and will pursue us with all His might. Sometimes, God allows us to get through to the other side of the protective gate in our heart to get a full dose of what we think we need. We then return kicking and screaming and complaining, even act like a 2 year old; but God always provides shade for us, He gives us the desires of our hearts, and He gives us sound discipline...

Within hours I was back on the street, wandering aimlessly, knowing what to do and doing the opposite anyway. I knew my marriage was over. I knew I could possibly die. I knew that I was putting

myself in harms way. For 3 solid days I was
lost...BUT GOD...

PART THREE

HUMILITY

Stepping back over the threshold of Jacob's Well Recovery Center for Women

PART THREE
TABLE OF CONTENTS

43 – *Stepping Into Serenity*

June 22nd – 2014 – Day 2 – Well, here I am, back at Jacob's Well. After feeling like I had lost everything, I surrendered AGAIN. When I got home to an empty, dark house and realized my husband had left, I wanted to run back into the arms of the enemy. I'm so grateful I had no gas in my car and no money to my name or I would have. Why did I give up so easily? Hindsight is always 20/20 and after I replayed every single conversation and moment leading up to the decision to relapse into destruction, I saw the devil's schemes played out like a well organized stage performance with a script written just for me. He got me with the good things. I filled myself to capacity with positive, productive things and lost my relationship with God. I began to do everything in my own strength. Quiet time was quick and rushed and I sure wasn't still long enough to listen to what God had to say to me. I had it ALL figured out. I was following through with what I thought His plan for me was, and no one could tell me otherwise. The harder you climb, the further you fall, and that is so true. I don't feel so much like I failed...I just made a mistake. It's what I chose to do after the mistake that will show my true character.

Proverbs 24:16 - for though the righteous fall seven times, they rise again, but the wicked stumble when calamity strikes.

I feel like God put on the brakes to what I thought I needed and He brought me home. There was so much going on prior to my going back to the street. His mom died, he cleaned out our bank account in Kentucky, work was draining, finances were tight, writing became a chore, and I was exhausted all the time.

My dependence on God had diminished and I was dependent solely on my husband. I had a choice to make when I arrived home after 3 days with no sleep and a broken heart. I could run away back to the death that awaited me, or I could humble myself before God and allow the good people of Jacob's Well to take me home to learn balance, how to listen to God, how to slow down, how to find peace again, and how to live.

This is God's way of showing me Who is in charge. What an amazing opportunity for me to be reminded of Who my first love is, Jesus. It's time to lay my plans to the side and allow God to truly have His way.

2 Corinthians 1:9 - Indeed, we felt we had received the sentence of death. But this happened that we might not rely on ourselves but on God, who raises the dead. Psalm 40:2 - He lifted me out of the slimy pit, out of the mud and mire; he set my feet on a rock and gave me a firm place to stand.

As I am about to turn in for the night, the Lord tells me to read:

John 10:12 – The hired hand is not the shepherd and does not own the sheep. So when he sees the wolf coming, he abandons the sheep and runs away. Then the wolf attacks the flock and scatters it.

I was relying on man alone and not the Shepherd to get me through tough times. No wonder the wolf attacked. I was standing alone.

June 24th – 2014 – Day 4 – I woke up this morning feeling oppressed and weak – physically, spiritually, and emotionally. I have unending feelings of guilt and shame and I am plagued by nightmares of all the things I left behind to come back here. There are so many disappointments. I had the thought this morning that I couldn't do this again – another 6 months. Worry and anxiety flooded my soul like a long, deep crevice of darkness that has no light inching its way into every fiber of my being.

2 Chronicles 15:7 – But as for you, be strong and do not give up, for your work will be rewarded.

Any person is subject to blame, including myself, if I cannot reconcile myself to the fact there is sin. I am not innocent, but I thank God that I am forgiven. That is what I need to remember as I trudge through the days ahead. There IS a light at the end of this dark tunnel.

Isaiah 41:10 – So do not fear, for I with you; do not be dismayed, for I am your God. I will strengthen you and help you; I will uphold you with my righteous right hand.

There were once 639 laws which were broken down by God and made into the 10 commandments, all of which have been broken by me, at least in my heart. Jesus made it even more simple.

Matthew 22:36-39 – "Teacher, which is the greatest commandment in the law?" [37] Jesus replied: "'Love the Lord your God with all your heart and with all your soul and with all your mind.' [38] This is the first and greatest commandment. [39] And the second is like it: 'Love your neighbor as yourself.'

That's it. If I follow these two simple commands, all else will melt away. Perfect Love Drives Out Fear. As I am lying down for the night, yet again the Lord speaks to me and tells me to read

Zechariah 3:2 - The LORD said to Satan, "The LORD rebuke you, Satan! The LORD, who has chosen Jerusalem, rebuke you! Is not this WOman a burning stick snatched from the fire?"

45 – *Never Give Up*

June 29th – Day 8 – I made it through my first seven days. This has been a very humbling and emotional week, but the best is yet to come. God has a wonderful future in store for me. Sometimes it is hard to see the forest for the trees, but God is sovereign and His plans are not dictated by my action. Even when evil wanted me dead, God had a plan for my misery and my pain. Even though my choices led me back here, there is still much to learn and understand. God is not done with me yet. God has stripped me of my marriage, my home, my car, my possessions, but He is still with me.

Philippians 4:12-13 - I know what it is to be in need, and I know what it is to have plenty. I have learned the secret of being content in any and every situation, whether well fed or hungry, whether living in plenty or in want. 13 I can do all this through him who gives me strength.

He has removed my desire for stuff but is still providing for my every need. I am a fighter. It's time to stop licking my wounds and get back in the battle.

Susan did her sermon this morning at church, "Life Goes On". Susan Brogan, you will not read this until 6 months from now, but your sermon this morning put me on a new path that I didn't think was possible. It is a path that I used to start down but got too scared because guilt and shame would shackle me to the gate leading up to the path. It is a path that I used to believe I was really on, but never truly was. It is a path of reality and complete surrender. I'm not in a full sprint yet, but I've taken the first step out of the gate.

Thanks to beautiful people like yourself and this new journey I am on and the trust I have toward you and Jesus, I can walk and not crawl.

God is the God of what I have, of what I lost, and of what I have left.

46 – *Silence*

July 6th – 2014 – Day 15

Proverbs 21:23 - Those who guard their mouths and their tongues keep themselves from calamity.

Sometimes I talk way too much. I say things out of turn and without thinking and then wish right away that I had a muzzle on my mouth. Then follows sometimes hours and even days of trying to fix what popped out of my unbridled tongue. You know, God requests that I enter into solitude with Him, to cease the striving of human effort, and give Him my undivided attention. That can most definitely take place in quiet times, but it doesn't have to be limited to just set aside time. I can rest in silence and withdraw from the demands in the company of others so I can hear his voice over the noise of my own thoughts BEFORE they become words. I have a crazy need to control things, so why can't I control my mouth? I can if I just allow myself to be silent and let God have His agenda. I learned this lesson the hard way yesterday. God cannot transform me if I keep my beak in motion.

Proverbs 17:28 - Even fools are thought wise if they keep silent, and discerning if they hold their tongues.

47 – My Beating Heart

July 9th – 2014 – Day 18 - I am acutely aware of my heart beating inside my chest. I can put my hand there, close my eyes, and picture the chambers moving in perfect succession to one another, blood pumping from one chamber to the next and flowing freely through my veins, giving life as it passes through each article of my being. I am also acutely aware that the spiritual part of my heart that I cannot see is broken. It isn't shattered beyond repair, but the band-aid I keep putting on it continues to get ripped off and there is a deep wound that can only be healed by one gentle touch from my Savior.

Everything that I do, every decision that I make, every word that I speak, comes from the heart and when it is broken, then my actions are also broken. Hurting people hurt people. When am I going to really get that memo? The life blood that flows through me needs to be pure and the only way for that to be so is to allow the craziness to surface so that I can receive healing.

Numbers 13:31-33 (NIV) - But the men who had gone up with him said, "We can't attack those people; they are stronger than we are." 32 And they spread among the Israelites a bad report about the land they had explored. They said, "The land we explored devours those living in it. All the people we saw there are of great size. 33 We saw the Nephilim there (the descendants of Anak come from the Nephilim). We seemed like grasshoppers in our own eyes, and we looked the same to them."

I face some pretty heavy giants in my life, but when I allow their size and stature to create fear, then I lose sight of what I know about God. I forget about trust, patience, forgiveness, acceptance, and compassion. I was a bit distracted the other week because I failed to see the promise right before my very eyes because I was still so focused on the journey ahead which included facing giants. You know, the past is already gone. When I force my will on God, I end up back in the wilderness, plain and simple. Fear and self-loathing then become my BFF's again and I forget... Rebellion begins with dissatisfaction, then complaining, bitterness, and resentment. Oh, what a tangled web we weave. Being discontnent with what I already have will cause me to lose it without gaining what I desire the most. My wasted efforts in trying to prove my heart to those who could care less about it and keeping up appearances would have been much better spent on finding God's answers to my troubling situation. HELLO?!?!?!

Mark 5:25-34 (NIV) - And a woman was there who had been subject to bleeding for twelve years.26 She had suffered a great deal under the care of many doctors and had spent all she had, yet instead of getting better she grew worse. 27 When she heard about Jesus, she came up behind him in the crowd and touched his cloak,28 because she thought, "If I just touch his clothes, I will be healed."
29 Immediately her bleeding stopped and she felt in her body that she was freed from her suffering. 30 At once Jesus realized that power had gone out from him. He turned around in the crowd and asked, "Who touched my clothes?"
31 "You see the people crowding against you," his disciples answered, "and yet you can ask, 'Who touched me?'"

32 But Jesus kept looking around to see who had done it. 33 Then the woman, knowing what had happened to her, came and fell at his feet and, trembling with fear, told him the whole truth. 34 He said to her, "Daughter, your faith has healed you. Go in peace and be freed from your suffering."

My situation is not impossible. My heart beats for the promises of God, even when I can't see the answers. Patience is a beautiful heart virtue that symbolizes trust and I'm patiently learning patience. Fear can no longer crush the life blood of Jesus that flows through my beating heart, but I first have to face reality and allow healing to begin.

48 – *Downfall of Pride*

July 15th – Day 24 - I'm learning very quickly that pride is my biggest downfall. You would think that ego wouldn't continue to get in the way of nearly everything I try to do, but it does.

Have you ever seen a car wreck? It's as if everything is moving in slow motion, although your brain is functioning and you see what is happening so clearly, metal crashing into metal, smoke and tires spinning, it is wrong. But there is nothing at all that you can do to stop it. You know that it's going to hurt either yourself or someone else. You are helpless. That's how I feel in regards to the sin of pride. I know exactly when pride entered my life when it began to form a deep root that spread its tentacles to the parts of my heart that I didn't know existed. It was when my dad went to prison and everything I thought I knew about life, family, trust, love, hope, and security went out the window and pride, justification, humiliation, confusion, doubt, insecurity, rejection, fear, self-loathing, and anger flew in - all at the ripe old age of 11.

The thing about pride today in my life is I recognize it, I see it, I know it is there, I can feel it sending its poison from the deep root up to the surface and forming lies in my mind but before I know it, I speak or act and then it is too late. I have a wreck. I begin to rely on my own skills and strength in whatever situation I find myself in and I begin to misjudge...everything.

Joshua 7:10-12 (NIV) - The Lord said to Joshua, "Stand up! What are you doing down on your face? 11 Israel has sinned; they have violated my covenant, which I commanded them to keep. They have taken some of the devoted things; they have stolen, they have lied, they have put them with

their own possessions. 12 That is why the Israelites cannot stand against their enemies; they turn their backs and run because they have been made liable to destruction. I will not be with you anymore unless you destroy whatever among you is devoted to destruction.

I was made liable to destruction because I was unwilling to learn my lesson and remove pride from my life. It's a sneaky little sucker. It is actually the base from which most of my decision that are out of whack jump from. God has explicit commands. Remove anything that hinders.

Galatians 5:7-9 (NIV) - You were running a good race. Who cut in on you to keep you from obeying the truth? 8 That kind of persuasion does not come from the one who calls you. 9 "A little yeast works through the whole batch of dough."

I am sinful and He alone is Holy. If I run to Him BEFORE opening my big mouth, I might can avoid the inevitable crash.

Proverbs 16:18 (NIV) - Pride goes before destruction, a haughty spirit before a fall.

49 – *Defining Character*

July 25th – Day 33 - Webster defines "character" as one of the attributes or features that make up and distinguish an individual.

In attempting to define my character, I am realizing that my attributes are my strengths, but also my weaknesses. God has perfect character because He is holy, trustworthy, and unchanging. He created me in His image at the beginning of time in order to love and hold me and walk with me in and through life. I was made to see God face to face. It was the first sin that cast us all out and made us different. In defining my own character, I realize that my sins and my circumstances changed my character along the way to righteousness.

I was born to live for God and to trust Him, so I believe God is refining me through the difficult circumstances I find myself in so that He can stretch me and further develop my character. He wants to see my capacity to trust and obey my Perfect Creator. I can't walk with God when there are still parts of my makeup that need to be tested. I am reminded of artists who draw caricatures of people. They attempt, in a few short strokes of a pencil, to capture the true essence of a person. Most times we laugh at the distorted view of ourselves because we are covering up the fact that the artist hits the nail on the head. It becomes hard to look at our misconstrued face which shows a funny side to our inward flaws. However, this is no laughing matter. I have to constantly look at my real face in a mirror and say, "This is who I am, God. Please make me more like You."

Here goes - me in a nutshell - I would say that I am a serious individual. I don't like games. There is a time for work and that seems to be all the time for me. I'm a bit judgmental and critical but the flaws I see in others are often a reflection of myself. I have a tendency to let jealousy and bitterness take root in some aspects of my life and it taints everything in an instant. I tend to be self-righteous and through that horrible characteristic I end up losing compassion and humility. I have major control issues. I'm known to be a tad selfish and very impatient. I'm rebuking all of those things right now in Jesus' name. I can't change what I don't acknowledge.

FIFTY – *Pain in the Offering*

AUGUST 4th – 2014 – Day 43 – Church service rocked me to my core today. When the Lord peels away the layers of my onion, it feels as if my heart is being ripped from my chest. Some things I try to hold on to so tight until He has no other option than to remove it from me and show me what it really looks like. Reality is a hard pill to swallow. I was broken. I looked down at my hands after surrendering all at the altar and saw the hands of an innocent child who was once to grow up and live out dreams. I was a shy little girl with so many questions and so many confusing disappointments but also so many accomplishments. I was broken by the world at such a vulnerable age and because of it, I broke everyone who loved me. The godly sorrow that flooded my being, my soul, and my spirit yesterday was the culmination of everything lost along the way.

2 Corinthians 7:10 - Godly sorrow brings repentance that leads to salvation and leaves no regret, but worldly sorrow brings death.

The Lord stripped me down to the bare bone then told me to raise my hands in praise for all He is about to do. Promises are worth waiting for and there is pain in the offering. I am so grateful for this breaking. I am grateful for the trust the Lord places in me with this pain. I am going to praise Him through it all. Seeing my situation from His perspective hurts and I am so unworthy of His love but I am FORGIVEN.

Acts 1:7-8 - He said to them: "It is not for you to know the times or dates the Father has set by his own authority. 8 But you will receive power when the Holy Spirit comes on you; and you will be my witnesses in Jerusalem, and in all Judea and Samaria, and to the ends of the earth."

51 – *Relentless Pursuit*

August 9th – 2014 – Day 48 - Asa spoke today in devotion and something so profound that it took my breath away. He said, "Beware of what you become in pursuit of what you want." He left us to talk amongst ourselves on that topic and the girl next to me said she had never really pursued ANYTHING, but she had. Like countless other women at Jacob's Well she pursued with all her might, relentlessly, the drugs and lifestyle that nearly killed her.

Sometimes we pursue things that aren't originally on the table, things that are completely new and foreign, sometimes positive things that still distract us from our purpose. Both she and I lost ourselves in the process of the relentless pursuit.

2 Chronicles 15:7 (NIV) - But as for you, be strong and do not give up, for your work will be rewarded.

As for me, in my pursuit for happiness, I lost my pursuit of the One Being that makes the world turn. I lost God and became self-righteous.

2 Chronicles 12:1-2 (NIV) - After Rehoboam's position as king was established and he had become strong, he and all Israel with him abandoned the law of he Lord. 2 Because they had been unfaithful to the Lord, Shishak king of Egypt

attacked Jerusalem in the fifth year of King Rehoboam.

We open ourselves up for attack when we forget where our blessings come from. Rehoboam, the king of Judah, did make an attempt to follow God in a fallen world, but as he peaked in popularity and power, he abandoned God and ran in his own strength. When everything is going right, that is when I need to guard my faith closely and steer clear of self-sufficiency. Confession and humility open the door to receiving mercy. When I leave God out of my life and my plans, I lose myself spiritually. Outer beauty has to come from inner strength and the only way to be strong is to seek the Lord in ALL my pursuits.

2 Chronicles 14:11 (AMP) - Asa cried to the Lord his God, O Lord, there is none besides You to help, and it makes no difference to You whether the one You help is mighty or powerless. Help us, O Lord our God! For we rely on You, and we go against this multitude in Your name. O Lord, You are our God; let no man prevail against You!

The army against me is mighty, but God is stronger. I have to recognize my limitations in order to do the best I can and allow Him to do the rest.

2 Chronicles 15:2 (NIV) - He went out to meet Asa and said to him, "Listen to me, Asa and all Judah and Benjamin. The Lord is with you when you are with him. If you seek him, he will be found by you, but if you forsake him, he will forsake you."

I will never have to face anything alone. When I look for God in the midst of the moment, it goes against the grain of the world. As long as I stay in the Word, absorb His teaching, and turn back to Him, the enemy is defeated in every pursuit.

James 4:7-10 (MSG) - So let God work his will in you. Yell a loud no to the Devil and watch him scamper. Say a quiet yes to God and he'll be there in no time. Quit dabbling in sin. Purify your inner life. Quit playing the field. Hit bottom, and cry your eyes out. The fun and games are over. Get serious, really serious. Get down on your knees before the Master; it's the only way you'll get on your feet.

52 – *Beautiful Burden*

August 11th – 2014 – Day 50

Psalm 41:1-2 (NIV) - Blessed are those who have regard for the weak; the Lord delivers them in times of trouble. The Lord protects and preserves them—they are counted among the blessed in the land—he does not give them over to the desire of their foes.

I had the opportunity to run the camera at church recently and what I saw through that lens changed by entire perspective on Jacob's Well Ministries. The floodgates of gratitude were opened up. As the end of the service drew near, Susan made an altar call for those who needed to let go of the weight of un-forgiveness. She said, "When we carry un-forgiveness we are tired, we are burdened, and we are carrying around on our back all those who hurt us."

Usually, I am the first person down at the altar in moments of sweet release and surrender, but I was bound by my service and unable to move. So I quietly observed. What the Lord showed me through the tiny lens changed everything. I saw a lot of hurting women, a sea of tears dropping to the floor, hands raised in surrender, and chains breaking. I heard the cries of the desperate, a loud wail of deliverance, and I saw captives walking out of jail cells of their own making. I saw some doubled over from the pain of release, and some kneeling in reverent awe. On the altar stood my friend; I saw her surrounded by the multitude and for the first time I understood her beautiful burden, the responsibility laid on her by God to bear witness to the people and help the Lord raise up an army. Every single person at that altar is a soldier in training, each of them following now the Commander of the Heavenly Host!!

As tears were streaming down my face and neck, I was completely overcome with a plethora of emotions. God is LOVE. I was reminded of the prophet, Jeremiah. He was sick, unable to eat, tired, and ridiculed; but, he was always doing God's will to speak truth into the lives of the people inhabiting his beloved city. "Turn back from your wicked ways, PLEASE! I am begging you!" would be his cry over and over and over again.

> *Jeremiah 29:10-14 (NIV) – This is what the Lord says: "When seventy years are completed for Babylon, I will come to you and fulfill my good promise to bring you back to this place. 11 For I know the plans I have for you," declares the Lord, "plans to prosper you and not to harm you, plans to give you and hope and future. 12 Then you will call on me and come and pray to me, and I will listen to you. 13 You will seek me and find me when you seek me with all your heart. 14 I will be found by you," declares the Lord, "and will bring you back from captivity. I will gather you from all the nations and places where I have banished you," declares the Lord, "and will bring you back to the place from which I carried you into exhile."*

He was set apart by his mission for God, but he was also one of them. His burdensome love for Jerusalem made him cringe everytime he spoke of what was to come. All the people had to do was listen to God and obey. But they didn't. They were marched right out of the streets of their beloved home and right back into captivity. The beautiful women of Jacob's Well have a choice, as do I. Follow the leader, or go back into slavery, yet still so many choose the easy way out. Don't do that. Live in a way that is difficult, but so very worth it!

Psalm 42:5 (NIV) – Why, my soul are you downcast? Why so disturbed within me? Put your hope in God, for I will yet praise him, my Savior and my God.

53 – *Faith and Reason*

August 13th – 2014 - Day 52 - Sometimes I think things to death. I analyze every thought regarding a situation, turning it over and over in my brain in an attempt to make it all fit. I start looking at it from every angle and from different viewpoints to the point where I can't distinguish my voice from God's voice from satan's voice. I begin to start asking myself a million questions only to be given answers...by myself.

Ezra 8:21-23 (MSG) - 21-22 I proclaimed a fast there beside the Ahava Canal, a fast to humble ourselves before our God and pray for wise guidance for our journey—all our people and possessions. I was embarrassed to ask the king for a cavalry bodyguard to protect us from bandits on the road. We had just told the king, "Our God lovingly looks after all those who seek him, but turns away in disgust from those who leave him." 23 So we fasted and prayed about these concerns. And he listened.

A situation happened recently, in the middle of a fast, when out of the blue one conversation opened my eyes to a completely foreign perspective and the floodgates flew open. Instead of asking God for guidance and direction right away, I used my measly flesh between my ears and stumbled through thought after thought, question after question, trying to make sense of it all. Faith and Reason then went on a journey with me, something they should never do...together.

Reason told me logically the course of action and that I should stay put. Faith led me along the rugged path, pushing me into realms unseen and showed me promises along the way. Reason told me to make a pros/cons list, Faith told me to step out even though it seemed impossible. Reason told me to settle for the easy road, Faith told me to take the road less traveled and to never give up. I pray that God will find a way to distinguish His voice from all the other chatter. In the meantime, I will claim that there is no way I can make this trip without Him. I need His protection. I know what God's promise is for me and I know that it doesn't include allowing any human to put themselves in position to be a roadblock (ex-husbands to be exact). God blessed me with people in my life and entrusted them to my care and being selfish and bowing out isn't on the docket for me, not today. Everything from Him is for His use and if I move on then I am essentially taking for granted His precious gifts.

Isaiah 61:7 (NIV) - Instead of your shame you will receive a double portion, and instead of disgrace you will rejoice in your inheritance. And so you will inherit a double portion in your land, and everlasting joy will be yours.

Everlasting joy AND a double portion in place of my disgrace? Sign me up! I believe I will follow Faith on this journey down the road. It may eventually lead me to the place where Reason took a detour, but for today I am ok with the questions that are looming, unanswered. The road is long, the journey difficult at best. This is a marathon, not a sprint.

Psalm 5:8 (AMP) - Lead me, O Lord, in Your righteousness because of my enemies; make Your way level (straight and right) before my face.

54 – *The Harvested Crops*

October 11ᵗʰ – 2014 – Day 111 – Last night, I had the opportunity to minister to one of my sisters out of my own pain. She is struggling and a once battle-ready warrior princess is now sitting in the bunker, her war paint smeared from her tears. I know her pain; I feel her hurt. I sense her indecision and believe for her when she can't see the forest for the trees. When I shared with her about the situation with my boys, it blessed me to see a new perspective float across her vision. When we consistently follow Him with deepest sincerity and expectation, He WILL bless us.

> *Joel 2:25 - "I will repay you for the years the locusts have eaten—*
> *the great locust and the young locust,*
> *the other locusts and the locust swarm—*
> *my great army that I sent among you.*

My crops and her crops that we harvested long ago were eaten by the massive swarm. Our fields lay empty. We have sat aside our children and our dreams have died, to us, but not to God. He promises restoration. I have to remember in the process of waiting that I am God's servant. I am NOT His advisor. Hope surrounds me – the consistent expectation of what is to come.

> *2 Corinthians 4:16-17 - Therefore we do not lose heart. Though outwardly we are wasting away, yet inwardly we are being renewed day by day. ¹⁷ For our light and momentary troubles are achieving for us an eternal glory that far outweighs them all.*

55 – *My Reality*

October 17th – 2014 – Day 117

**Habakkuk 1:2 - *How long, LORD, must I call for
help,
but you do not listen?
Or cry out to you, "Violence!"
but you do not save?***

I am so grateful I woke up from the nightmare I had last
night. satan has no new tricks up his sleeve so he tries
to get me in my sleep. I woke up, but the real
nightmare in my life is still raging around me. Reality is
setting in that my husband made a choice to leave his
recovery center without a plan, without a purpose, and
without godly counsel. The Lord has been preparing me
slowly for the revelation that came before the
separation.

He is removing things from my life so I depend upon
Him solely. It seems my husband was but a seasonal
person in my life, someone sent to teach me something
about myself. Getting caught up on what MIGHT
happen will cause me not to see what COULD happen.
Sometimes I feel like God is playing a game of chess
with my life, stragically moving pieces around on a
board and knocking some off – one at a time.

**Habakkuk 1:5 - *Look at the nations and watch—
and be utterly amazed.
For I am going to do something in your days
that you would not believe,
even if you were told.***

I am so angry right now at the time wasted. I am sick
and tired of going around the same mountain. I was
told the grim news yesterday by Pastor that sealed my

fate as a married woman of an addict. What is accepted will be repeated and I'm too tired to keep up this charade.

Habakkuk 2:1-4 -
I will stand at my watch
and station myself on the ramparts;
I will look to see what he will say to me,
and what answer I am to give to this complaint.
Then the LORD replied:
"Write down the revelation
and make it plain on tablets
so that a herald may run with it.
3 For the revelation awaits an appointed time;
it speaks of the end
and will not prove false.
Though it linger, wait for it;
it will certainly come
and will not delay.
4 See, the enemy is puffed up;
his desires are not upright-
but the righteous person will live by his
faithfulness.

God is closing mighty doors in my face and I stand alone in this hallway. The only other door open for to run into is the own leading me closer to Jesus. He will no longer delay. His timing is impeccable. I am going to trust Him, even when I don't understand the events as they unfold around me. When God speaks and people move, He speaks with clarity. He has the power to move nations. Even if I stand alone in this hall, a door to my future closed before my very eyes, and everyone around me is falling away, I am still going THAT way, toward the ONLY lover of my soul, my Savior.

Habakkuk 3:17-19 – Though the fig tree does not
bud and there are no grapes on the vines, though

the olive crop fails and the fields produce no food, though there are no sheep in the pen and no cattle in the stalls, 18 yet I will rejoice in the Lord, I will be joyful in God my Savior. 19 The Sovereign Lord is my strength; he makes my feet like the feet of a deer, he enables me to tread on the heights.

56 – *Inconsistent Obedience*

October 19th – 2014 – Day 119 - Someone dear to me asked me today, "Hasn't he always been there for you when YOU messed up?" Well, sure he has, but at what point is enough, ENOUGH?? I'm ready to get off this crazy train. Maybe the time has not yet come for him to rebuild his house, his holy temple.

Haggai 1:5-9 - Now this is what the Lord Almighty says: "Give careful thought to your ways.⁶ You have planted much, but harvested little. You eat, but never have enough. You drink, but never have your fill. You put on clothes, but are not warm. You earn wages, only to put them in a purse with holes in it." ⁷ This is what the Lord Almighty says: "Give careful thought to your ways. ⁸ Go up into the mountains and bring down timber and build my house, so that I may take pleasure in it and be honored," says the Lord. ⁹ "You expected much, but see, it turned out to be little. What you brought home, I blew away. Why?" declares the Lord Almighty. "Because of my house, which remains a ruin, while each of you is busy with your own house.

I am not being judgmental in saying that my future ex-husband is working in the flesh and not in the spirit. That is by far an observation only. But here is the thing. Contamination rubs off on others so easily and I will not be contaminated by the shaking of THIS nation.

Fear of the unknown is a choice. It is a decision. Today, I choose to stand in truth and grace. I am responsible before God for my actions. I cannot use my environment as an excuse to sin. I am free to make a choice to change my life and blaming others isn't an option anymore. I am tired of repeating the mistakes of others. Only God can heal me by the blood of Jesus shed for my sins on the Cross, but I have to be willing.

I am being tested and tried and my heart is broken into a thousand pieces. My need for immediate action is overwhelming, but I must stand still and that is my strength. You know, ALL my filthy clothes are replaced with robes of righteousness after being snatched from the fire, so what in the world would ever make me want to turn back and look in the opposite direction for relief? Love? Is THAT love that I am walking away from? I don't think so. Change is painful, but it's absolutely necessary in order to inherit the promises.

> *Zechariah 3:2-7 - The Lord said to Satan,*
> *"The Lord rebuke you, Satan! The Lord, who has chosen Jerusalem, rebuke you! Is not this man a burning stick snatched from the fire?"*
> *3 Now Joshua was dressed in filthy clothes as he stood before the angel. 4 The angel said to those who were standing before him, "Take off his filthy clothes."*
> *Then he said to Joshua, "See, I have taken away your sin, and I will put fine garments on you."*
> *5 Then I said, "Put a clean turban on his head." So they put a clean turban on his head and clothed him, while the angel of the Lord stood by.*
> *6 The angel of the Lord gave this charge to Joshua: 7 "This is what the Lord Almighty says: 'If you will walk in obedience to me and keep my requirements, then you will govern my house and have charge of my courts, and I will give you a place among these standing here.'*

Susan says that when people leave, let them. That is exactly what I am doing because I can't stand to see that years with this man were for nothing. I guess he needs a full dose of whatever he thinks he wants and that obviously isn't me. Inconsistent obedience cannot produce consistent blessings and I am tired of being inconsistent. He chose not to heed the warnings from godly people in his life and now he is desolate. My cause for action is now very plain and I stand and wait on deliverance.

**Zechariah 10:12 – "I will strengthen them in the Lord
and in His name they will live securely,"
declares the Lord.**

57 – *Unbelief*

October 31st – 2014 – Day 131

Mark 10:17-22 - As Jesus started on his way, a man ran up to him and fell on his knees before him. "Good teacher," he asked, "what must I do to inherit eternal life?" 18 "Why do you call me good?" Jesus answered. "No one is good—except God alone. 19 You know the commandments: 'You shall not murder, you shall not commit adultery, you shall not steal, you shall not give false testimony, you shall not defraud, honor your father and mother.'"
20 "Teacher," he declared, "all these I have kept since I was a boy."
21 Jesus looked at him and loved him. "One thing you lack," he said. "Go, sell everything you have and give to the poor, and you will have treasure in heaven. Then come, follow me." 22 At this the man's face fell. He went away sad, because he had great wealth.

I am a hoarder and a selfish one at that. I do that when I feel backed into a corner and I don't know when my next "fix" will come. It's survival mentality. It's street mentality. Lately, I have been hoarding food and money. People are blessing me left and right; yet, I still hoard and hold on to for dear life what I think is rightfully mine. It takes me back to the street when I would be at the end of my money train and would hold on for hours to the last hit like my life depended on it, because at the time, it did.

I am in a safe place right now and all my needs are met, so why am I hoarding? Why am I being so selfish with what has been given to me? Why won't I share with my

less fortunate sisters? Because I have UNBELIEF.
There is a part of me that know the bank account is
empty because in the middle of his recent relapse he
stole everything. There is no one to care for me and I
am scared. I don't want to believe that the Creator of
the ENTIRE UNIVERSE can care for my needs and
wants and desires. I want to believe.

*Mark 9:24 - Immediately the boy's father
exclaimed, "I do believe; help me overcome my
unbelief!"*

58 – *Lost Sheep*

November 7th – Day 138

Luke 15:3-7 - *Then Jesus told them this parable: 4 "Suppose one of you has a hundred sheep and loses one of them. Doesn't he leave the ninety-nine in the open country and go after the lost sheep until he finds it? 5 And when he finds it, he joyfully puts it on his shoulders 6 and goes home. Then he calls his friends and neighbors together and says, 'Rejoice with me; I have found my lost sheep.' 7 I tell you that in the same way there will be more rejoicing in heaven over one sinner who repents than over ninety-nine righteous persons who do not need to repent.*

I was a lost sheep. I wasn't REALLY lost. I chose to leave the gate to go after self-pity and shame. I knew to do good, but I couldn't do it. I was exhausted from being content with mundane tasks, from nurturing and loving people who wronged me on a daily basis. I was tired of walking around pretending as if everything was in my little field while my heart was being ripped in two.

So, I did what I always do when the going gets rough and I ran away from the peaceful meadow, right into the arms of the wolf.

God places a very high value on me. He created me for His purposes and I wasn't fulfilling it. When I chose another path, God came chasing after me diligently. He rejoiced when I was found! I was beyond hope, but He came for me anyway. He drew me close to Himself in order to deepen my peace, in order to give me rest. He did it so that I would be of greater use to the other sheep in the pen.

59 – *The Puppet*

November 23rd – 2014 – Day 154

> **Romans 4:18-21 - Against all hope, Abraham in hope believed and so became the father of many nations, just as it had been said to him, "So shall your offspring be." [19] Without weakening in his faith, he faced the fact that his body was as good as dead—since he was about a hundred years old—and that Sarah's womb was also dead. [20] Yet he did not waver through unbelief regarding the promise of God, but was strengthened in his faith and gave glory to God, [21] being fully persuaded that God had power to do what he had promised.**

Against all hope. I feel like a puppet, attached to a bunch of strings with Christ as my Puppeteer. Along the way, some of my strings have been broken and extensions of myself have fallen away, yet I am still able to move. I can walk, talk, work, move around with ease. I can sing and dance if that is what the Puppeteer desire that I do and for that alone I am grateful. However, I am still very much aware of the frayed edges of the strings that hang sadly over my head. Can I ever to THAT? Will the Creator of my marionette form ever choose to take me to His shop and attach those strings that I desire to have back?

If I continue to look at the circumstances surrounding the strings, then I have NO REASON to expect God to fulfill His promises. If I continue to gaze with longing as the world does, then I will fall away into unbelief and eventually cut off the other life sustaining threads.

Today, I rely with confidence on His Word. He is waiting to send His help in the form of wood workmanship and patient deliverance at the time of my greatest need, when all seems impossible so His hand will be plainly seen in my repair. I have been controlled by many puppeteers in my life, but for once, even in my broken state, I will wait on the promises of God. I will wait for the rest of my earthly life if need be.

SIXTY – *Love*

November 28th – 2014 – Day 159 – Love. It is the greatest gift from our perfect Creator. It set in motion our entire planet. It is why life was created and it is the reason we were formed from dust to walk around in unity. Nothing matters without love.

I am so grateful for the gifts that God has bestowed upon me, but what good are they if I don't use them in love? It is the center of my being. Do I get confused at times when God asks me to make major adjustments in my life? Sure. But I must quickly dispel that because God is not the author of confusion. Do I get angry some days at having to be obedient? Absolutely! But God is not the author of anger either. Do I get dog tired of running a race that most days seems to have no finish line in sight? More times than I can count. But that, too, is from the enemy. Exhaustion is a tool used to make me ineffective. I have to put selfishness, pride, and childish ways behind me in order to move forward in His grace.

1 Corinthians 13:1-13 - If I speak in the tongues of men or of angels, but do not have love, I am only a resounding gong or a clanging cymbal. 2 If I have the gift of prophecy and can fathom all mysteries and all knowledge, and if I have a faith that can move mountains, but do not have love, I am nothing. 3 If I give all I possess to the poor and give over my body to hardship that I may boast, but do not have love, I gain nothing.

4 Love is patient, love is kind. It does not envy, it does not boast, it is not proud. 5 It does not dishonor others, it is not self-seeking, it is not easily angered, it keeps no record of wrongs. 6 Love does not delight in evil but rejoices with the truth. 7 It always protects, always trusts, always hopes, always perseveres.
8 Love never fails. But where there are prophecies, they will cease; where there are tongues, they will be stilled; where there is knowledge, it will pass away. 9 For we know in part and we prophesy in part, 10 but when completeness comes, what is in part disappears. 11 When I was a child, I talked like a child, I thought like a child, I reasoned like a child. When I became a man, I put the ways of childhood behind me. 12 For now we see only a reflection as in a mirror; then we shall see face to face. Now I know in part; then I shall know fully, even as I am fully known.
13 And now these three remain: faith, hope and love. But the greatest of these is love.

Faith, the foundation; and hope, the attitude must align perfectly for LOVE to be set in motion.

I'm angry today at a hater, someone in my life who went from friend to enemy overnight. I'm angry at someone I trusted without knowing that her own insecurities had her looking upon me with scorn and without my knowledge.

Without faith (knowing and believing God's promises for my life), and hope (confident expectation in the things unseen), I would NOT be able to love her regardless of her feelings. I would slip easily into selfish behaviors because of the reflection I see in the mirror of her eyes when I see her face to face. Without love, I would shrink away and take on the insecurities of another without thought.

Today, I am able to see past the mirror and look in the promise, for ME, which is eternal life where all my gifts and talents given to me will pass away and all that will be left is love. Today, I choose to use our differences to give God the glory! I praise Him for making us both unique!

1 Corinthians 16:13 - Be on your guard; stand firm in the faith; be courageous; be strong.

61 – The Dark

December 15th – 2014 – Day 176 – I walked around in the dark for a very long time, convinced it was where I belonged, where I deserved to be. Good and evil looked the same. I carried so much hate in my heart, mainly toward myself, that everything that was supposed to be beautiful was ugly, and everything ugly was beautiful – just like Susan said. I was hiding something all the time, living in secret and keeping to myself.

It wasn't until the Light of Truth was brought before me and the demons that had taken over my life were forced to flee. Darkness cannot exist in the presence of pure and holy Light and to say that the powerful source made stripping my old self off very uncomfortable is an understatement.

Change is painful. Being exposed for who I really was in that life was painful. The best news is Jesus was uncomfortable too. He already knew all about me, even when I claimed to know Him and lived for my selfish desires anyway and became the hypocrite I always despised, He was there. He knew and loved me anyway.

1 John 1:5-7 - This is the message we have heard from him and declare to you: God is light; in him there is no darkness at all. 6 If we claim to have fellowship with him and yet walk in the darkness, we lie and do not live out the truth. 7 But if we walk in the light, as he is in the light, we have fellowship with one another, and the blood of Jesus, his Son, purifies us from all sin.

62 – *Hypothesis*

December 18th – 2014 – Day 179

Revelation 3:8 - I know your deeds. See, I have placed before you an open door that no one can shut. I know that you have little strength, yet you have kept my word and have not denied my name.

This past 6 months has truly been a test, a laboratory of sorts. One thing after another has come against me, yet I still walk toward my purpose even when I am weak. So many days I have longed to stay in bed and sleep until the cows come home. So many days I have refused to put pen to paper, yet I do it anyway. So many times I have wanted to just throw my hands up and give up and hide in a corner but I didn't.

A hypothesis is a tentative assumption made in order to draw out and test the logical consequences. It is an interpretation of a practical situation or condition taken as the ground for action. My silly assumption is that I can go anywhere and do anything without my unseen Creator as my guide.

God isn't some big man in the sky, checking off a naughty or nice list. He is as close to me as my own breath. If He is so close, of course He knows my every move. If He knows my every move, then He knows the struggles I face, the thoughts that race, what happens before, during, and after I wake up. He knows the fear, the triumphs, the mountains, and the valleys. He knows the exhaustion, the love, the discord, and the doubt. He knows ME. He created me before time and shouted my name in heaven to the angelic host awaiting the announcement of my arrival.

What am I to do with this proof that comes directly from the Word of God? What actions are required for me to walk through the open door? What is on the other side? Does it really matter as long as it is His will? All I have to do, even in my weakness, is walk - because He sees, and He knows.

PART FOUR

GRATITUDE

My New Life In Christ

PART FOUR
TABLE OF CONTENTS

63 – *Today*

I wrote this Sunday morning upon awakening. I have been struggling the past few days with feeling the pressure of front line ministry. I expected attacks, but I did not expect them to come from inside of me. I was looking for them to come from everyone else, and I continued to blame everyone else, but I was really the problem. Granted, the ministry of Jacob's Well has a huge promotion coming in the Kingdom of God and the attack is on every single staff member and everyone involved. I am so grateful to just be a part of what is taking place in the spiritual, but if I take my OWN self out, then what?!?!? Here is what I wrote yesterday morning as my spirit was searching for truth. I had NO IDEA that God would confirm nearly every single sentence and thought and prayer before the end of the day Sunday through people, through music, through sermons handed to me by others, through prayer, and through the Word of God. God is so amazing and His love for me is endless and He never ceases to amaze me. Here is a piece of my heart...

1 Samuel 13:6 (AMP) – When the men of Israel saw that they were in a tight situation – for their troops were hard pressed – they hid in caves, holes, rocks, tombs, and pits or cisterns.

I am not hiding ANYMORE. With huge blessings comes even greater opposition. So much has taken place over the past week that my head is spinning. It has been great, it's been good, bad, and outright ugly. Panic wants to set in, but no one here is having that. We are all standing on the edge of a cliff, the enemy is fastly approaching from behind, having caught up with us, even to the point of wounding some. I have a choice to make, succumb to the pressures or jump off the cliff in blind faith knowing full well that we will be caught by the Lord.

Psalm 91:11-12 (NIV) – For he will command his angels concerning you to guard you in all your ways; 12 they will lift you up in their hands, so that you will not strike your foot against a stone.

I'm reminded that God's will is supreme over all. He can deliver us in ways unimaginable. He can save us, even from ourselves. I am my own worst enemy. I make conscious decisions to sabotage the good right before my very eyes. With everything going on, I expect opposition; however, I did not see it coming from inside of me. I did not calculate that my own crazy thinking would have me lying down in front of my very own bus. When I allow stressful situations to get to me, my old friends come for an unwelcome visit. Paranoia is the first to arrive, wreaking havoc on my psyche. Then comes in anxiety, confusion, jealousy, anger, fear, pride (both the positive and negative connotations...YIKES!), and last but not least, doubt. I don't know why I am surprised.

Matthew 12:43-45 (NIV) - "When an evil spirit comes out of a man, it goes through arid places seeking rest and does not find it. 44 Then it says, 'I will return to the house I left.' When it arrives, it finds the house unoccupied, swept clean and put in order. 45 Then it goes and takes with it seven other spirits more wicked than itself, and they go in and live there. And the final condition of that man is worse than the first."

They came knocking and I opened the door. It was my choice. I was a clean vessel and the stress of this pioneer effort opened the just a crack for these ugly spirits to come back. I can't imagine how the American Pioneers felt. They walked into territories never before seen, stepped foot onto land already occupied by foreigners, but they continued to walk. They pushed forward. They faced persecution, arrest, natural disasters, exhaustion, and major opposition from every angle, but they walked. Where would we be if they hadn't persevered? Where will the people coming behind ME be if I don't persevere?

2 Corinthians 4:8-10; 17-18 (NIV) – 8 We are hard pressed on every side, but not crushed; perplexed, but not in despair; 9 persecuted, but not abandoned; struck down, but not destroyed. 10 We always carry around in our body the death of Jesus, so that the life of Jesus may also be revealed in our body. 17 For our light and momentary troubles are achieving for us an eternal glory that far outweighs them all. 18 So we fix our eyes not on what is seen, but on what is unseen, since what is seen is temporary, but what is unseen is eternal.

Deuteronomy 8:1-18 (NIV) - Be careful to follow every command I am giving you today, so that you may live and increase and may enter and possess the land the Lord promised on oath to your ancestors. 2 Remember how the Lord your God led you all the way in the wilderness these forty years, to humble and test you in order to know what was in your heart, whether or not you would keep his commands. 3 He humbled you, causing you to hunger and then feeding you with manna, which neither you nor your ancestors had known, to teach you that man does not live on bread alone but on every word that comes from the mouth of the Lord. 4 Your clothes did not wear out and your feet did not swell during these forty years. 5 Know then in your heart that as a man disciplines his son, so the Lord your God disciplines you.

6 Observe the commands of the Lord your God, walking in obedience to him and revering him. 7 For the Lord your God is bringing you into a good land—a land with brooks, streams, and deep springs gushing out into the valleys and hills; 8 a land with wheat and barley, vines and fig trees, pomegranates, olive oil and honey; 9 a land where bread will not be scarce and you will lack nothing; a land where the rocks are iron and you can dig copper out of the hills. 10 When you have eaten and are satisfied, praise the Lord your God for the good land he has given you. 11 Be careful that you do not forget the Lord your God, failing to observe his commands, his laws and his decrees that I am giving you this day. 12 Otherwise, when you eat and are satisfied, when you build fine houses and settle down, 13 and when your herds and flocks grow large and your silver and gold increase and all you have is multiplied, 14 then your heart will become proud and you will forget the Lord your God, who brought you out of Egypt, out of the land of slavery. 15 He led you through the vast and dreadful wilderness, that thirsty and waterless land, with its venomous snakes and scorpions. He brought you water out of hard rock. 16 He gave you manna to eat in the wilderness, something your ancestors had never known, to humble and test you so that in the end it might go well with you. 17 You may say to yourself, "My power and the strength of my hands have produced this wealth for me." 18 But remember the Lord your God, for it is he who gives you the ability to produce wealth, and so confirms his covenant, which he swore to your ancestors, as it is today.

TODAY, I am taking back my land! I am pioneering to a place never before dreamed! I am sweeping out my house and filling it again with the goodness of Christ! I will not be shaken! I am a strong warrior, I am highly favored, I am a weapon against opposition! No longer will I fall under the weight of scrutiny! No longer will I lay down! I am going to the darkness to bring others out and I will not be moved! satan has games but I'm not playing paddy cakes anymore! The land belongs to Christ and He is allowing me and my fellow brothers and sisters to lay siege to it and conquer it for generations to come. We will fly the flag of Christ and we will walk under His banner into the promised land. Today we fight. Today we reclaim what the enemy stole long ago. I'm so grateful to the people in my life who care about me enough to point out the pitfalls, who don't allow me to fly under the radar and simply exist. They push me out of complacency and into the light of painful truth. Looking at myself before taking the jump off the cliff is absolutely necessary. If my ego jumps with me, I'm destined to perish. TODAY...I'm taking my destiny back!

64 – *Fisher of Men*

I was such a prissy little girl. I only wore dresses and frilly little socks with patent leather shoes. When I finally got past my fear of the big farm house in the middle of nowhere that the dinosaurs must have built, I decided to go spend the weekend with the man who hung the moon, my Papaw, the apple of my eye. He and Mamaw were so old fashioned that they slept in different rooms. I couldn't have been more than 8 years old. We all retired to bed early after watching golf on a blaring TV because Papaw couldn't hear and refused to get hearing aids. We all went to our own corners of the big house, Papaw in his room in the back, Mamaw and I cuddled in the front bedroom where my mom used to sleep. Round about 4:30am, I felt someone nudging me. "Julie Anne, where are your playclothes?!? JULIE ANNE!! Wake up and tell me where your playclothes are!" Papaw had gone through my little red suitcase that said, "Going to Grandmas" and found my only playclothes: dresses, frilly socks, and patent leather shoes. When I told him that as I wiped the sleep from my eyes, his exasperated sigh said it all.

The next thing I knew, he had handed me a cup of his special "kid coffee" (milk, sugar, and a splash of coffee for flavor), and bundled me up in his old pickup truck and we were off to Kmart, lumbering down the long driveway before the sun. He purchased for me with his meager wages a pair of blue jeans, a t-shirt, and some tennis shoes and we were off. Once I was donned in proper "Papaw attire" that was more than uncomfortable, we went fishing. The beauty that surrounded me at Cypress Lake took my breath away. I could hear the birds singing their morning song in the cypress trees that grew right out of the lake, the squirrels chased each other from tree to tree, and the fish were hopping in the warm water sustained by the rising sun. My Papaw put creepy, crawly critters on the end of my line and taught me how to cast. And we caught fish!! His proud smile warmed my heart each time I looked into his shining blue eyes for approval. On more than one occasion, I caught my line in a tree. "We aren't fishing for squirrels, Julie Anne!" we the patient words from a loving man as he cut my line time and again. The rest of that sunny day, we golfed from his homemade fairway and hole (I hit a hole in one in the field behind the house), we bowled, and we drank Shirley Temples on the porch swing. Me and Papaw! Two peas in a pod!

Jesus is so patient with me too. He wants to walk in fields with me, sit on a quiet lake, and look at me with proud, loving eyes. He cuts my fishing line and lets things loose that don't belong, branches caught that symbolize wrong people that can't hold the weight of responsibility. He calls me to fish in His lake breeming with souls ready to be pulled into His boat. My Papaw would be so proud! Today, I am a fisher of men!!!

Mark 1:16-17 – As Jesus walked beside the Sea of Galilee, He saw Simon and his brother Andrew casting a net into the lake, for they were fishermen. "Come, follow me", Jesus said, "and I will send you out to fish for people."

65 – *God is Impartial*

Ruth 1:16 (HSCB) – But Ruth replied: Do not persuade me to leave you or go back and not follow you. For wherever you go, I will go, and wherever you live, I will live; your people will be my people, and your God will be my God.

Imagine this...I am standing outside the beautiful gates of heaven, the pearls that adorn it are bigger than the trunks of hundred year old oak trees and they shimmer in the Light that seems to come from nowhere, yet everywhere. As the gates swing open in a wide arc, I take my first step onto a street made of gold that is so brilliant in all its luster that I am paralyzed by the sight. The colors that surround me are not of earth, beautiful hues never before seen by human eyes. In my ear, I can clearly hear the prayers of the saints in every single earthly language...and the SINGING!!!

It's as if I am standing center stage at the largest opera house in the universe and there stand millions of singers, their voices lifted in harmonious perfection and praise to their Savior who sits high on the throne ahead of me. The angels are soaring overhead and around the throne of Light and their wings beat in unison to the music and create a breeze that blows against my face...the Mighty Wind of God...and touches me like a sweet kiss.

I then hear my name that sounds like thundrous waves crashing into my heart. The next thing I hear in my spirit that tears me from the perfection I have always sought is this:

Matthew 7:21-23 (NIV) - "Not everyone who says to me, 'Lord, Lord,' will enter the kingdom of heaven, but only the one who does the will of my Father who is in heaven. 22 Many will say to me on that day, 'Lord, Lord, did we not prophesy in your name and in your name drive out demons and in your name perform many miracles?' 23 Then I will tell them plainly, 'I never knew you. Away from me, you evildoers!'"

What a miserable legacy to leave. What a terrible way to end my life. I may be a sinner, but I am forgiven because of the sacrifice Jesus made for me at Calvary. I am a blood bought precious daughter of a King, but I don't need to walk around acting like my life is perfect and judging others for their imperfections, donning my crown and acting better than the rest.

What would have happened if Naomi had placed judgement on Ruth for her messed up past, her pagan family, her ways of doing things? Ruth would not have met Boaz, and they would have not become the ancestors to Christ Himself. Food for thought...you may not understand a person, but to sit in judgment over them is now your demise, regardless of your deeds for the kingdom. That hurts me to know that I have some things I need to work on in my own life in this very area. I am so unworthy of the beautiful, constant, unchanging love that I receive, so why I am so hesitant to give it? Ruth left everything; her home, her family, her gods; to follow Naomi and to follow the Lord. We all leave a lot in order to do the same.

God offers grace in the middle of bad circumstances and we ALL find ourselves broken in this fallen world. So who am I to put unrealistic expectations on my brothers and sisters who are just trying to walk this thing out the best way they know how? I found compassion last night in the most unlikely of ways, in the middle of my own pain, knee deep in circumstances that I can't control.

I have been praying for more compassion, and last night I FELT the pain of another human soul that was longing to be different and I loved her through it. God was not impartial to Ruth, He even made her an ancestor to the King. He is not impartial to any of us if we are willing to approach the throne of Light and Grace with humility.

1 Corinthians 13:4-7 (MSG) - Love never gives up. Love cares more for others than for self. Love doesn't want what it doesn't have. Love doesn't strut, Doesn't have a swelled head, Doesn't force itself on others, Isn't always "me first," Doesn't fly off the handle, Doesn't keep score of the sins of others, Doesn't revel when others grovel, Takes pleasure in the flowering of truth, Puts up with anything, Trusts God always, Always looks for the best, Never looks back,
But keeps going to the end.

Who are you going to love on today? Don't you want your crown in heaven that you can throw at the feet of our precious King?

66 – *Armor of God*

I think it's funny that satan tries to attack me mostly in my sleep. It shows what a coward he is. When I wake up, I absolutely have to go directly to the Word and put on my armor. Every single day. If I don't, then he will keep coming at me and hitting me upside the head with his stupid two-by-four. I learned quickly that I have the power to change my attitude, my circumstances, and my entire well-being by speaking words of truth into my life. Beth Moore says it perfectly: "God is not looking for spiritual giants. He is looking for believers who believe for a change."

Psalm 145:18 – The Lord is near to all who call on him, to all who call on him in truth.

Truth is the key that will bring me into victory. But I can't start speaking truth over myself until I am armed for battle.

Ephesians 6:10-17 – Finally, be strong in the Lord and in his mighty power. 11 Put on the full armor of God, so that you can take your stand against the devil's schemes. 12 For our struggle is not against flesh and blood, but against the rulers, against the authorities, against the powers of this dark world and against the spiritual forces of evil in the heavenly realms. 13 Therefore put on the full armor of God, so that when the day of evil comes, you may be able to stand your ground, and after you have done everything, to stand. 14 Stand firm then, with the belt of truth buckled around your waist, with the breastplate of righteousness in place, 15 and with your feet fitted with the readiness that comes from the gospel of peace.. 16 In addition to all this,

take up the shield of faith, with which you can extinguish all the flaming arrows of the evil one. 17 Take the helmet of salvation and the sword of the Spirit, which is the word of God.

It says FULL armor, not a piece, not just one thing, but ALL of it. As Susan says all the time, "What's in ALL? Everything! What's left out of ALL? Nothing!" The only way I can stand up against this terrible enemy that wants me dead is to stand my ground, armed and ready for battle. I must depend on God's strength and use every single piece He has given me. These enemies will try everything to turn me away from Jesus and back to sin. But God will not allow that to happen. Especially if I do my part and hit the floor ready for the onslaught.

I will stand FIRM in truth, righteousness, readiness, peace, faith, and salvation!! The belt of Truth will combat the lies. The breastplate of Righteousness will guard my heart since everything flows from it. My feet will be ready, not to run, but to STAND firm in what I believe! The shield of Faith will protect me from the flaming arrows that are being shot at me with all my past mistakes and my insecurities. Faith is believing in things unseen and I do believe! The helmet of salvation will protect my mind from the inner voice that plagues me. I have been saved through Christ Jesus. That is TRUTH.

I pray every day that the word of God is a sword coming from my mouth! I pray that He uses me in a way that I can speak to others clearly and without confusion as to the saving power of Jesus Christ.

2 Corinthians 10:3-4 – For though we live in the world, we do not wage war as the world does. 4 The weapons we fight with are not the weapons of the world. On the contrary, they have diving power to demolish strongholds.

Romans 8:18 – I consider that our present sufferings are not worth comparing with the glory that will be revealed in us.

67 – Battlefield in the Mind

2 Samuel 7:18-19, 28-29 (NIV) - Then King David went in and sat before the Lord, and he said: "Who am I, Sovereign Lord, and what is my family, that you have brought me this far? 19 And as if this were not enough in your sight, Sovereign Lord, you have also spoken about the future of the house of your servant—and this decree, Sovereign Lord, is for a mere human!" 28 Sovereign Lord, you are God! Your covenant is trustworthy, and you have promised these good things to your servant. 29 Now be pleased to bless the house of your servant, that it may continue forever in your sight; for you, Sovereign Lord, have spoken, and with your blessing the house of your servant will be blessed forever."

I was recently put in a different type of leadership position, one I wasn't mentally prepared for, and one I didn't seek God's face in. The battle in my mind ensued and I opened the (meaning I MADE A CHOICE) and allowed things to settle in my spirit that didn't belong. I gave myself over to the enemy; hook, line, and sinker. Feelings of worthlessness, fear, worry about what others were thinking, anxiety, and paranoia took over and I then forgot to pray. I turned off the switch to my power source and sank into oblivion. I was afraid to ask anyone to do anything, I felt like everyone was talking about me, and then I realized that this crippling affect happens every single time God promotes me. Why can't I get THAT memo? I then dove head first into "work mode" and forgot to love others. Compassion flew out the window with the wind.

You know, in reading about David in 2 Samuel, I have come to see that God forgives, He doesn't hold grudges, and He promotes for His glory, not mine. David was a sinner, through and through, but he was a man after God's own heart.

Acts 13:22 (NIV) - *After removing Saul, he made David their king. God testified concerning him: 'I have found David son of Jesse, a man after my own heart; he will do everything I want him to do.'*

David pleased the people of Israel because he tried to please GOD. THAT is where the light in me and the leadership should come from. The praise of people isn't important. Striving to do right in the eyes of God is what will earn respect and trust. Each time I show generosity and compassion, my character is strengthened and good decisions are made without thought. My feelings are NOT a reliable guide for moving through life.
Boy, am I grateful for those who see me acting out, but they don't discount me. Today is a new day. The Lord's mercy and grace are brand new. Thank you, Lord, for another chance to get it right in YOUR eyes. I want to be a woman after God's own heart. Lord, continue to show me Your way.

68 – *Did You Forget?*

You know, the struggle is real. So many of us want to put on masks to hide from the world how we really feel. I know for me, I become fearful in being so transparent because I am afraid people will think I am weak, that they will judge me, that my transparency will open a for vulnerability. But I have learned over these past several months to rip off the mask and expose the schemes of the enemy so it loses its power over me. The longer I hold things in, the more it festers and causes sores within me.

The women read forgiveness letters at Jacob's Well the other day. As I listened intently to their wails as they read through tears, some of them forgiving their parents for the wrongs they had to endure as children, I heard the voices of my own children saying the same things to me in the spirit and I was overcome with emotion.

I wrote this within minutes of the last letter being read:

"Have you forgotten about me, God? I feel forgotten. It's been a long time. I miss them so much. I know You were there when my world fell apart. I know I spoke a blessing over my family before I allowed the darkness to consume me and I know when I said, "God is going to take care of us" before my eyes were veiled from Your Truth that You heard me. I know You heard me because my family prospered and I survived so I know You heard me. I know that You allowed me to suffer so that I could bring You glory, so where are You today? Where were

You yesterday? Where are You now? Did You Forget? What about them? What about THEM, God? Do they hate me? Do they think about me when they lay their heads down at night? Do they know what I look like or do they even care that I am still alive? Do their hearts ache for me ever? Do they wonder? Do they know You? Do they know what You promised me? Do they believe it? What do they sound like? What games do they like to play? What are their favorite pastimes and what do they like to eat? When they skin their knees on their tall lanky legs, do they wish I was there to kiss it and make it better? I WANT TO SCREAM!! How much longer? I'm willing to wait, God, and I am being so patient! I am listening for Your voice but all I hear today is crickets. I have a lot of good words, God. I have a lot of things that you tell me to say. I push aside myself and give myself away for You every day, so why do I feel forgotten??? I LOVE YOU, Lord. I understand that your ways are not my ways. I can't even begin to think like you think. Please don't tarry long, O Lord."

I was immediately taken to Job 38-42. Below are some things that brought tears to my eyes and I was instantly repentant.

Job 38:1-11 (MSG) - And now, finally, God answered Job from the eye of a violent storm. He said:
2-11 "Why do you confuse the issue?
Why do you talk without knowing what you're talking about?
Pull yourself together, Job!
Up on your feet! Stand tall!
I have some questions for you,
and I want some straight answers.
Where were you when I created the earth?

Tell me, since you know so much!
Who decided on its size? Certainly you'll know that!
Who came up with the blueprints and
measurements?
How was its foundation poured,
and who set the cornerstone,
While the morning stars sang in chorus
and all the angels shouted praise?
And who took charge of the ocean
when it gushed forth like a baby from the womb?
That was me! I wrapped it in soft clouds,
and tucked it in safely at night.
Then I made a playpen for it,
a strong playpen so it couldn't run loose,
And said, 'Stay here, this is your place.
Your wild tantrums are confined to this place.'

It goes on and on with God questioning Job....Then...

Job 40:1-14 (MSG) – 1-2 God then confronted Job
directly:
"Now what do you have to say for yourself?
Are you going to haul me, the Mighty One, into
court and press charges?"
3-5 Job answered:
"I'm speechless, in awe—words fail me.
I should never have opened my mouth!
I've talked too much, way too much.
I'm ready to shut up and listen."
6-7 God addressed Job next from the eye of the
storm, and this is what he said:
"I have some more questions for you,
and I want straight answers.
8-14 "Do you presume to tell me what I'm doing
wrong?
Are you calling me a sinner so you can be a saint?
Do you have an arm like my arm?
Can you shout in thunder the way I can?

Go ahead, show your stuff.
Let's see what you're made of, what you can do.
Unleash your outrage.
Target the arrogant and lay them flat.
Target the arrogant and bring them to their knees.
Stop the wicked in their tracks—make mincemeat
of them!
Dig a mass grave and dump them in it—
faceless corpses in an unmarked grave.
I'll gladly step aside and hand things over to you—
you can surely save yourself with no help from me!
Job 42:1-6 (MSG) – 1-6 Job answered God:
"I'm convinced: You can do anything and
everything.
Nothing and no one can upset your plans.
You asked, 'Who is this muddying the water,
ignorantly confusing the issue, second-guessing my
purposes?'
I admit it. I was the one. I babbled on about things
far beyond me,
made small talk about wonders way over my head.
You told me, 'Listen, and let me do the talking.
Let me ask the questions. You give the answers.'
I admit I once lived by rumors of you;
now I have it all firsthand—from my own eyes and
ears!
I'm sorry—forgive me. I'll never do that again, I
promise!
I'll never again live on crusts of hearsay, crumbs of
rumor."

Do you know what happened then? If you go on to read and I highly suggest that you do, God restored to Job everything that he had lost.

Job 42:10-15 (MSG) – 10-11 After Job had interceded
for his friends, God restored his fortune—and then
doubled it! All his brothers and sisters and friends

came to his house and celebrated. They told him how sorry they were, and consoled him for all the trouble God had brought him. Each of them brought generous housewarming gifts.

12-15 God blessed Job's later life even more than his earlier life. He ended up with fourteen thousand sheep, six thousand camels, one thousand teams of oxen, and one thousand donkeys. He also had seven sons and three daughters.

God will restore. In His time, in His way, His perfect plan. Who am I? He didn't forget.

69 – *Directionally Challenged*

How many of us walk around in circles? We are unsure of where to go, how to get there, what road to take, which voice to listen to. The enemy wants us confused and off the beaten path.

There was a time not so long ago, 3 days after I stepped across the threshold of Jacob's Well Ministries for the first time, when I begged them to pull out a map and show me where on the planet I was. I was completely oblivious to my whereabouts and it nearly drove me insane. To me, nothing feels worse than not knowing where I even exist on this small blue earth. What a terrifying feeling for the control freak I used to be.

I am not directionally challenged in the physical realm anymore. I use my I phone maps nearly everywhere I go, even if I already know the way. It's the sense of false security I get in the desperate hope of not getting lost since I am so easily distracted. I beg others to use the app that can get you anywhere and will speak to you in the accent of your choice just so I don't have to tell them directions on how to get to my location. I still get lost in the spiritual, because I forget to listen to the still, small voice.

Isaiah 30:21 (NIV) - Whether you turn to the right or to the left, your ears will hear a voice behind you, saying, "This is the way; walk in it."

I have a very dear friend who I recently introduced to "Maps" share a funny story with me. He said, "I knew how to follow the blue line, but I did not know that you could hit 'START' and the voice would tell you exactly which turn to take." Upon that revelation, God gave me one of His own. The Lord spoke to me and said, "Isn't that just something? My people get distracted by phone calls or text messages as the drive the path I intended for them and they in turn, without thinking, go off the trail with the blue line which points them in the way to go. Other distractions lead them to dead ends, through needless traffic stops because they are moving too quickly out of haste, and off cliffs because they have sabotaged themselves and no longer even care about the road they were traveling. None of them hit 'START' which would have opened their ears to hear My Voice beckoning them and showing them the way to go with ease."

WOW! How many times have we only thought we were doing right just by following the blue line and then allowed the enemy ample time to get into our weary minds on long journeys into the middle of seemingly nowhere where God's promise awaited us? We aren't always supposed to know where we are going, but God offers us His direction. All we have to do is ask. Are you going to hit the "START" button today and give yourself a break from trying to do everything in your own strength?

Psalm 119:1-8 (MSG) - 1-8 You're blessed when you stay on course, walking steadily on the road revealed by God. You're blessed when you follow his directions, doing your best to find him. That's right—you don't go off on your own; you walk straight along the road he set. You, God, prescribed the right way to live; now you expect us to live it. Oh, that my steps might be steady, keeping to the course you set; then I'd never have any regrets in comparing my life with your counsel. I thank you for speaking straight from your heart; I learn the pattern of your righteous ways. I'm going to do what you tell me to do; don't ever walk off and leave me.

SEVENTY – *The Narrow Gate*

Matthew 7:13-14 - Enter through the narrow gate. For wide is the gate and broad is the road that leads to destruction, and many enter through it. 14 But small is the gate and narrow the road that leads to life, and only a few find it.

There is but one way. And it isn't always easy. People always talk about not being able to see the forest for the trees. Every time I hear that, I envision myself back at Jacob's Well, the place where found freedom in Christ and was set free from my bondage. The house sits on a piece of property, flat, and grassy. Right next to and on the other side of the turtle pond sits a row of dense forest and tree canopies. The fog that sometimes comes up over the tree line makes the forest look like it is on fire, especially in the early morning or late afternoon as the sun sets. It's so beautiful, but also awesome and mysterious. As I see myself standing there in the openness of the field, completely vulnerable and naked to the firmament above me, I ponder those trees. As I hear a dog barking through the trees, attempting to grab a snare a not so unsuspecting squirrel or other varmint with the obnoxious bark, I long to be just a flea on his fur in order to be able to see the forest for what it is.

What is on the other side? What does it really look like if only I were able to look past the trees? There is narrow gate. It is the <u>only</u> way to Christ and out of the billions of people who live on the planet, a very small remnant actually decides to take that small path into the woods to follow their Savior in to unchartered territory, following the Light of Salvation into realms unseen, into the darkness, into the fog. The path can become overgrown, weeds can overtake the humbleness of it all. It can be choked off by the very life that sustains the rest of the earth. It's up to ME to continue forward, allowing Christ to shine His Light on one step, then another. Before long, after the loss of everything, after walking alone, after countless vain attempts at taking the highway to destinations never intended for me, I chose the small path into the woods. All perspective changed in an instant and I stood before the Son of God in a beautiful meadow. Eternal life and love!

Matthew 10:39 - Whoever finds their life will lose it, and whoever loses their life for my sake will find it. Psalm 23:1-4 - The Lord is my shepherd, I lack nothing. 2 He makes me lie down in green pastures, he leads me beside quiet waters, 3 he refreshes my soul. He guides me along the right paths for his name's sake. 4 Even though I walk through the darkest valley, I will fear no evil, for you are with me; your rod and your staff, they comfort me.

71 – Hi, My Name is Julie

2 Peter 2:17-22 - These people are springs without water and mists driven by a storm. Blackest darkness is reserved for them. 18 For they mouth empty, boastful words and, by appealing to the lustful desires of the flesh, they entice people who are just escaping from those who live in error. 19 They promise them freedom, while they themselves are slaves of depravity—for "people are slaves to whatever has mastered them." 20 If they have escaped the corruption of the world by knowing our Lord and Savior Jesus Christ and are again entangled in it and are overcome, they are worse off at the end than they were at the beginning. 21 It would have been better for them not to have known the way of righteousness, than to have known it and then to turn their backs on the sacred command that was passed on to them. 22 Of them the proverbs are true: "A dog returns to its vomit," and, "A sow that is washed returns to her wallowing in the mud."

I'm about to get bold, but I am not apologizing for it. This is my opinion and how I feel about my OWN walk through addiction recovery. My feelings do not express those of anyone else I know and I commend any and all who are finding their own way out of their depravity. That being said...

I began my recovery process in anonymous rooms, surrounded by tradition and people who claimed over their own spirits on a daily basis that they WERE addicts or alcoholics. It never occurred to me that I could rain down blessings on myself by halting the words, "Hi, my name is Julie, and I AM an addict" and instead proclaiming, "Hi, my name is Julie, I fight from victory, and I am a redeemed and restored child of the Living King." I had no God in my life and bringing Him into my atheist home wasn't an option. If I couldn't bring Him home, I couldn't see bringing Him into my heart because it was completely foreign to me.

All I knew of my life before drugs and alcohol was religion, not relationship. My higher power in anonymous rooms then became the rooms themselves. I was religious about that, no doubt. People were staying clean, but so many were still living depraved lives; not all I must add, but some. I was barely escaping from my own hell and I was being led by people who were wrongdoers in their own flesh. I then traded those dark rooms for darker nights on the streets and darker moments in my heart and mind. I was a self-proclaimed addict and would always be one.

Each relapse sent me careening closer to death in a shorter amount of time each go around. When I found myself under the covering and teaching of Jacob's Well Ministries, I found a God and a Savior in Christ Jesus that was more than anything I could have ever imagined! The love and peace and knowledge that came flooding into my spirit changed the way I looked at life in general. I escaped the pollutions of the world through full awareness of the saving blood of Jesus, but I still became entangled in my flesh and my condition was worse than before. My heart was a jumbled mess on this last trip to hell and I longed to have never known about the Light of Truth. I had turned back from the Holy commandment given to me and I was broken seemingly beyond repair.

God is faithful and I am grateful for His love that never ends. It is only because of Christ that I am free today. I was a fool, I uttered my own loud boasts from pulpits designed to keep me in bondage. I enticed others to know of a higher power that had long ago been forgotten as Jesus Christ Himself through years upon years of traditions and laws that promised "freedom" without a Savior. His name was hidden behind self-liberty and I was enslaved to 12 steps and self-help. I desire with all that I am to see other people truly set free, not stuck at a wall that is unseen but very real. The walls CAN be broken only by the wrecking ball of true salvation! No other higher power created by man can ever compare. MY gratitude speaks when I care and share with others the GOSPEL...JESUS AS SAVIOR.

72 – The Beginning

Recently, a soon to be graduate of Jacob's Well came to me and spoke out of her mouth that she felt as if she were back at ground zero, back at square one, back at the starting point, unable to see clearly the path before her. Haven't we all been there? Lost? Back at the beginning? Looking upon a starting point wondering how in the world we got there? Her words to me sounded so negative, so I began to pray before speaking life into her. God reminded me quickly of the TRUE beginning.

Genesis 1:1-4 (NIV) - In the beginning God created the heavens and the earth. 2 Now the earth was formless and empty, darkness was over the surface of the deep, and the Spirit of God was hovering over the waters. 3 And God said, "Let there be light," and there was light. 4 God saw that the light was good, and he separated the light from the darkness.

Light meets the dark at our humble beginnings. We, as humans, are the ones who put such grand expectations on what should follow our starting point. You see, God didn't create the universe and our world out of NEED. He did so out of LOVE. So what we think we need is really miniscule in comparison to what God wanted from us from the beginning, which is Love. If I allow myself time to focus on the "What-If's" and get stuck in the "Should-Haves", I will forget the purpose set before me and I will choose to look solely to my past for answers.

I WILL GO INSANE and look for solitude in dark places. If I choose (AGAIN...It's all about my choices) to focus on the fact that I am NEVER alone, my past does not define my present, Jesus LOVES me, I stand on a solid rock, fear is not of the Lord, and God works everything out for those who love Him; then paranoia, fear, and depression must FLEE at the name of Jesus. I CHOOSE TO BELIEVE THE TRUTH.

The Spirit of God hovers over our waters in the beginning, even when the waves of uncertainty are so high and we are barely treading in the open sea. If God is Love, then Love is there, like a beautiful cloud forming over the tumultuous sea. Feeling as if you are back at the beginning of something is a fine place to start, because Love exists at the beginning of everything. Right?

We sometimes go through seasons and processes, some more painful than others, some shrouded by darkness, but remember, in the beginning, there was light, there was love, and there was God. Therefore, going backward, then, is no longer an option because the beginning is somewhere we have already been before, however uncomfortable it may feel.

We desperately need to lay aside the expectations of what "should" be, what life "should" look like, and find gratitude in the beginning because Light is there, Love is there, and God is there. We were all bathed in innocence when our lives were formed and we came into the world. Fellowship with our Awesome Creator God was broken due to our wilful disobedience. God has a plan for all of us, and the beginning is always a good place to start. Don't be discouraged today. Rest is at the starting line. Take a deep breath before venturing out and know that He already knows the process. In the beginning is where all good things happen.

73 – *The Rubber Band*

2 John 8 - Watch out that you do not lose what we have worked for, but that you may be rewarded fully.

Well, today I am feeling like I just need to crawl back in the bed. I feel like the whole world is against me and it's moments like these when I feel the most alone. I asked God this morning where He was and His response was, "Where are YOU?" I feel like a rubber band that gets heated as it is stretched. Each time the band is stretched it can go further and further as long as it is pulled slowly. Today, I feel like I am about to snap. I feel the tension and the pulling but there is no more give. If I offer suggestions, they are taken out of context. I feel like I'm on the plank ready to jump in shark infested waters but no one can see.

When I do all I can at the expense of myself, it is taken as selfishness. Everything seems to be wrong and nothing feels right. The crazy thing is I see that it is merely my own silly perceptions that have me stretched. I can't stay in this feeling long. It's time to step outside of myself and continue to help others in this race.

3 John 8 - We ought therefore to show hospitality to such people so that we may work together for the truth.

I may feel stretched and ready to snap at any minute, but there is always rest for the rubber band when God brings it back to its original position. He won't do that without my seeking Him for it. I am my own stumbling block, but I will not be moved, I will not be shaken, and the enemy will not win. Not today.

Jude 24-25 - To him who is able to keep you from stumbling and to present you before his glorious presence without fault and with great joy— 25 to the only God our Savior be glory, majesty, power and authority, through Jesus Christ our Lord, before all ages, now and forevermore! Amen.

74 – *Love and Legalism*

I had the awesome opportunity to witness firsthand a conversation where love reigned completely. The conversation started with a "Hello", as most do, and as it moved into deeper meaning, the reality of what was taking place brought me to my knees.

I overheard a broken woman who began the conversation with manipulative crying, a sort of begging for someone to listen through her tears. As she spoke, she realized that the old ways were not working for her in this moment, so the truth was revealed. Out of her own mouth came her intentions of what her plans were, how she was going to see to it that they came to fruition, and it was so brutally honest that it took my breath away. The person on the other end did nothing more than listen with an open heart without speaking or asking questions that would send the broken hearted person on the other end of the line deeper into paranoia and distrust.

As I listened, I was completely caught off guard. How dare this woman, who knows the right way to go, continue to live her life as if she were dying? How dare she ask for the things she was asking for instead of asking for the right kind of help? How dare she speak such hurtful things to the only person on the planet who is still fighting on her behalf? Who does this girl think she is? Why can't she just see? What in the world is she THINKING?

And then I saw it - the truest love I have ever seen was radiated through the phone toward this beat down individual who had originally called for tangible things to be handed to her so she could continue her spiral to self-destruction. The love of Christ poured forth and covered her ever so gently. Her questions were not answered the way she desired, but she hung up the phone and chose to make right decisions for her life, THAT day anyway. As Susan Brogan always says, "Love covers a multitude of sins." Never before had I really looked at myself long enough to see that I don't love enough. I am stuck between love and legalism. What a hard pill to swallow.

Romans 9:30-32 (NASB) – What shall we say then? That Gentiles, who did not pursue righteousness, attained righteousness, even the righteousness which is by faith; 31 but Israel, pursuing a law of righteousness, did not arrive at that law. 32 Why? Because they did not pursue it by faith, but as though it were by works. They stumbled over the stumbling stone.

Let me give you the definition of legalism. "Legalism is strict adherence, or the principle of strict adherence, to law or prescription, especially to the letter rather than the spirit; the doctrine that salvation is gained through good works; the judging of conduct in terms of adherence to precise laws."

That right there knocked me in the head. I didn't follow the laws for a very long time in my life. I didn't adhere to the laws of man or the spirit. I know what that feels like to live a life where every excuse in the book and every manipulative word that oozed from my mouth sounded better than the letter of the law. I was miserable. I see that misery on others, sad women who walk across the threshold of Jacob's Well, and I desperately want them to get out of their old ways of thinking so that they can see clearly the Light of Truth. But that isn't MY job.

I become a Pharisee when I expect others who are still trying to figure out how they got to where they are, if they are going to try this thing, and who to trust, to follow the letter of the law with precision. There is no script to this. The law is there, written in black and white for us all to see and be convicted by and turn from our ways.

Ephesians 4:22-24 – You were taught, with regard to your former way of life, to put off your old self, which is being corrupted by its deceitful desires; 23 to be made new in the attitude of your minds; 24 and to put on the new self, created to be like God in true righteousness and holiness.

Here is the thing. Some people were NOT taught how to live in Christ and have been living as just walking, breathing shells of people in this crazy messed up world their entire existence. However, I HAVE been taught, with regard to my former way of life. It's my responsibility to love people where they are, not to place judgment on them when they just don't know any better.

Jesus is the means by which we are convicted and brought to repentance. Not through Julie. Does it hurt me to see people completely stuck in deception and living lies? Yes. Does it hurt knowing that they are exactly where I used to be? Yes. Does it hurt seeing them slowly kill themselves in their mind, body, soul, and spirit? Yes. Can I do anything about it? Yes. I can love them.

Never before have I opened my spiritual eyes long enough to see what real Christ-like love looks like before I was afforded this front row seat to an amazing encounter that blew my mind into the stratosphere. As I sat there and listened intently to the conversation, I was immediately torn. Who am I really? What do I stand for, really? My desire is to be like Christ, not like a Pharisee who is following every letter of the law. I want to reach the broken, not push them away by my insistence on how they should behave. I want to love unconditionally, not judge. I still get it wrong, sometimes daily, but for the first time in my life, I see the truth. The truth hurts, but it will set you free.

1 Corinthians 13:4-13 (NIV) - 4 Love is patient, love is kind. It does not envy, it does not boast, it is not proud. 5 It does not dishonor others, it is not self-seeking, it is not easily angered, it keeps no record of wrongs. 6 Love does not delight in evil but rejoices with the truth. 7 It always protects, always trusts, always hopes, always perseveres. 8 Love never fails. But where there are prophecies, they will cease; where there are tongues, they will be stilled; where there is knowledge, it will pass away. 9 For we know in part and we prophesy in part, 10 but when completeness comes, what is in part disappears. 11 When I was a child, I talked like a child, I thought like a child, I reasoned like a child. When I became a man, I put the ways of childhood behind me. 12 For now we see only a reflection as in a mirror; then we shall see face to face. Now I know in part; then I shall know fully, even as I am fully known. 13 And now these three remain: faith, hope and love. But the greatest of these is love.

The good people of Jacob's Well loved me back to life when I was a dead woman walking in my own sins and transgressions. So who am I but a willing servant of the Most High God and I am called to LOVE.

1 Corinthians 15:56-57 (NIV) – 56 The sting of death is sin, and the power of sin is the law. 57 But thanks be to God! He gives us the victory through our Lord Jesus Christ.

75 – Resisting Temptations

I used to think that I could never be set free. Temptations would come at me and I would jump on them like they were running away with precious things of mine. I tackled temptation head on. Because it FELT GOOD to be bad. Silly, right?!?! I was so entangled by my sin, that I found pleasure in things that were killing me. It wasn't until the pain exceeded the pleasure that I realized there was something very, very wrong with me.

The pain of my consequences was there even while I was trying to seek pleasure. I was being haunted by the repercussions of my actions on a minute by minute basis. I was lost. I was hungry, I was angry, I was lonely, and I was tired. Time to HALT and seek the face of Jesus. Temptations are still there. The devil doesn't come to you with his red face and horns, he comes to you disguised as everything you ever wanted. That is truth! There is always an open door. It is a way out of every sticky situation we find ourselves in. Sometimes it isn't very easy to find, especially in our culture (or pit) of sin-inducing pressures.

1 Corinthians 10:12-13 – So, if you think you are standing firm, be careful that you don't fall! 13 No temptation has overtaken you except what is common to mankind. And God is faithful; he will not let you be tempted beyond what you can bear. But when you are tempted, he will also provide a way out so that you can endure it.

All temptation is common to ALL mankind, meaning I am not alone. I may feel like I am the only one going through things but it is COMMON to all man. So there are others who face temptations just as I do? I would be selfish to think it's all about me! But I have thought that way before. When we fail at things, or think we fail, we put pictures back up on the mud wall of our pits and decorate the floors with lavish rugs. Why?

Running from temptation is heroic in my eyes. I KNOW when I am being tempted. It's not a secret, I just pretend it is. The problem comes when I see the BIG open door with bells and whistles which lights up like the fourth of July in radiant colors! What I fail to see if I choose to walk through it is the tiny little door with its unpretentious frame, its modest handle, and its minimal adornments. That's my way out and sometimes it is uncomfortable, so I choose to stay stuck. However, we cannot stay where we are and go with God at the same time.

I would rather run in circles in a room with its big fancy door offering my temptation as long as I am running away than to step through it. Eventually I will find the right door because God says it is there and I believe His Word.

1 Thessalonians 5:23-24 – May God himself, the God of peace, sanctify you through and through. May your whole spirit, soul and body be kept blameless at the coming of our Lord Jesus Christ. 24 The one who calls you is faithful, and he will do it.

I live in a sinful world and evil is all around me. I can avoid tempting situations and concentrate on obeying God but I have to be able to put Him FIRST in all I do!! I have to stand in front of that beautiful door with its flashing lights and pray for Him to show me the way. And He will!

76 – *Shining the Light of Truth*

I want to live a life of honesty. I gotta tell you that honesty wasn't even possible or in my vocabulary when I was out there as a soldier for satan. Today, it's still a struggle. I have to sometimes catch myself then go back and make amends right away. Sometimes I lie to myself. It's when I shed the light of truth on the darkness that is trying to envelope me that I receive peace and hope yet again. Some things I don't like to talk about. I would love to be able to pretend that everything is OK. I have a reputation to uphold, right? I have people looking to me for a message every day, so I can't mess up...right? WRONG. I wish I were perfect, but the only perfect person that ever walked the face of the Earth was JESUS. I'm not perfect and I make mistakes. satan is very sneaky and he uses past behaviors to try to trip me up and the next thing I know I am back in depression, back feeling sorry for myself, back trying to do things in my own power and I start sliding down a very familiar slippery slope.

I was very good at pretending. I would get lost in what I "should" be and lose sight of where I really was. Last week was I was stuck in the breeding ground of the enemy. I nearly lost myself in the process of trying to work things out on my own. It wasn't until I RAN to Jesus and admitted my sin that I was able to be set free. I had a LOT to lay down that morning at church. My old patterns started creeping back in and unless I SPEAK TRUTH (even when it hurts and I am embarrassed) then I won't achieve freedom which is my greatest desire. I don't want to end up struck down because of my disobedience in trying to keep things under wraps.

JESUS KNOWS MY HEART. He knows what I do behind closed doors. He knows when old things (such as eating disorders and bad habits and depression) are knocking at my door to be let in. These things ask to be let in when I feel like I am losing control over important things in my life. Some things I HAVE let in. Here is what happened...those dark spirits in the recesses of my heart shrank back in the cowardly way that they only know how when the LIGHT of JESUS shone through at my request. MY REQUEST. I have to ask, or I won't receive! I have to be honest or it won't go away. I have to get REAL with myself and let God do His work in me or it won't work! I can't pretend. I can't walk around speaking in riddles and spinning a web of half truths. What happens to my character then?

Here is a prime example of dishonesty turned tragic when people don't speak truth:

Acts 5:1-11 - Now a man named Ananias, together with his wife Sapphira, also sold a piece of property. 2 With his wife's full knowledge he kept back part of the money for himself, but brought the rest and put it at the apostles' feet. 3 Then Peter said, "Ananias, how is it that Satan has so filled your heart that you have lied to the Holy Spirit and have kept for yourself some of the money you received for the land? 4 Didn't it belong to you before it was sold? And after it was sold, wasn't the money at your disposal? What made you think of doing such a thing? You have not lied just to human beings but to God." 5 When Ananias heard this, he fell down and died. And great fear seized all who heard what had happened. 6 Then some young men came forward, wrapped up his body, and carried him out and buried him. 7 About three hours later his wife came in, not knowing what had happened. 8 Peter asked her, "Tell me, is this the price you and Ananias got for the land?" "Yes," she said, "that is the price." 9 Peter said to her, "How could you conspire to test the Spirit of the Lord?

Listen! The feet of the men who buried your husband are at the door, and they will carry you out also." 10 At that moment she fell down at his feet and died. Then the young men came in and, finding her dead, carried her out and buried her beside her husband.

Jesus knows me. He KNOWS me!!! But it's ok because there is no condemnation in Christ Jesus! If I flat out lie to myself then I am only hurting myself! HE ALREADY KNOWS and He loves me anyway! He won't strike me dead and allow me to get my full dose of sin if I shine His light all over it! He'll pick me up, wipe me off, and make me clean as snow all over again! PRAISE THE LORD FOR MERCY AND GRACE!

1 John 3:20 – If our hearts condemn us, we know that God is greater than our hearts, and he knows everything. Romans 8:1-2 – Therefore, there is now no condemnation for those who are in Christ Jesus, 2 because through Christ Jesus the law of the Spirit who gives life has set you free from the law of sin and death.

WOO HOO!!!! Freedom never tasted so good!

77 – Good Morning World

As I sit here reflecting on the amazing ways God has touched me in the past year, I stand in awe. I am taken back to Friday morning this past week when I stood before my sisters in Christ and shared with them where I came from, how I allowed the enemy into my life, and how Jesus picked me up off the side of the road and pushed me in a direction I had never been before. The memories began to flood in like a swollen river and I was nearly overcome with emotion looking back on past mistakes. It was then that the revelation came that I want to share with you.

I was put on this earth for a purpose. It was Satan's job to get me out of line from that purpose and he did a pretty good job of it for a very long time. Each time a memory would come into my spirit, I would use it as an excuse to stay stuck. Good memories would come with guilt and shame. Bad memories would come with condemnation. Nothing in my memory served the purpose for which God called me to...until now. There is no condemnation in Christ Jesus (**Romans 8:1**) but I was condemned because I did not allow Christ into my heart.

I was hardened seemingly beyond repair.

Here is what I realized. God put Adam and Eve on the Earth as glorified humans whose only purpose was to love. He also gave them free will, because it would still be a choice whether or not to love the Creator who walked with them and talked with them and shared intimate moments with them. When the evil one came in and deceived Eve, free will reigned and they chose a wrong path. From that moment on, bad choices superseded obedience on more than one occasion and we fell into sin in the blink of an eye. However, there was always a small remnant who still believed.

Our brains are meant to filter out things that aren't used for the survival of our beings. Things come in and our brains shuffle through them like a deck of cards picking out the things we need for the day. Memories flood our conscience and those of us who have lived in active addiction for any period of time use them for death and not for life. God sets before us life and death, blessings and curses but it's up to us to choose. It's always about CHOICE.

I give satan way too much credit sometimes when memories come in and I call them "attacks". That is not what they are for. They are to remind me where I came from, so that I can survive the next time I am faced with a similar situation. I have no memory of being in my mother's womb, because I was surviving off of her. I have no memories of being a baby because, again, someone else what making sure I lived to see another day. The memories I have begin when I started making decisions that didn't seem like life or death at the time, but they were. I was making choices that would affect the outcome of the next day, and the next, and the next. My memories start when I started surviving. Here's the coolest part...God knew me and approved of me before I was born!

Jeremiah 1:5 (AMP) – Before I formed you in the womb, I knew [and] approved of you [as My chosen instrument], and before you were born I separated and set you apart, consecrating you [and] I appointed you as a prophet to the nations. Psalm 139:15-16 (NIV) – 15 My frame was not hidden from you when I was made in the secret place. When I was woven together in the depths of the earth, 16 your eyes saw my unformed body. All the days ordained for me were written in your book before one of them came to be.

WOW!!! Why can't I remember THAT?!?!? It's because if I could remember that place from which I came before being sent to the Earth to fulfil His purpose, I would AUTOMATICALLY choose Him because of the beauty of what I would see. There would be no free will and there would be no choice. My sole purpose is to love as Christ loves and as God loves and to convince others of the saving grace of our Father. We are meant to love and forgive. I am so grateful for the memories that come like a flood today because I CHOOSE to use them for His purpose in bringing others to His throne room!

Romans 8:28-32 (NASB) – 28 And we know that God causes all things to work together for good to those who love God, to those who are called according to His purpose. 29 For those whom He foreknew, He also predestined to become conformed to the image of His Son, so that He would be the firstborn among many brethren; 30 and these whom He predestined, He also called; and these whom He called, He also justified; and these whom He justified, He also glorified. 31 What then shall we say to these things? If God is for us, who is against us? 32 He who did not spare His own Son, but delivered Him over for us all, how will He not also with Him freely give us all things?

Now to the Book of Joshua. The entire nation of Israel had lost their first generation do to sin and desert wanderings. The adult children of the lost generation were standing at a flooded riverbank, the Jordan. They had seen miracle upon miracle right before their very eyes but this day they were scared, confused, doubtful, and insecure. Their leader, Moses, had died and now they were under the authority of someone new. They weren't sure how to trust. They were walking blind to a place where they had never been before on faith and a promise from a God they couldn't see. Sound familiar?? They were asked, on faith, to step into the swollen river which could easily take them under and the Lord promised to part the waters. As they stepped in; shaking from fear, grieving their loss, and exhausted from the trip; the waters separated and over a million souls walked into the promised land on a dry river bed. As the last person came into the new land flowing with milk and honey and stepped into a promise that should have been long forgotten, Joshua spoke:

Joshua 4:5-7; 21-24 (NIV) - "Go over before the ark of the Lord your God into the middle of the Jordan. Each of you is to take up a stone on his shoulder, according to the number of the tribes of the Israelites, 6 to serve as a sign among you. In the future, when your children ask you, 'What do these stones mean?' 7 tell them that the flow of the Jordan was cut off before the ark of the covenant of the Lord. When it crossed the Jordan, the waters of the Jordan were cut off. These stones are to be a memorial to the people of Israel forever." 21 He said to the Israelites, "In the future when your descendants ask their parents, 'What do these stones mean?' 22 tell them, 'Israel crossed the Jordan on dry ground.' 23 For the Lord your God dried up the Jordan before you until you had crossed over. The Lord your God did to the Jordan what he had done to the Red Sea when he dried it up before us until we had crossed over. 24 He did this so that all the peoples of the earth might know that the hand of the Lord is powerful and so that you might always fear the Lord your God."

Lay the stones down. Allow the memories to be used for God's glory and don't look back. Allow God to form new memories of things to come that have the ability to blow your mind if you can quiet it long enough to hear His voice.

78 – Things We Learned in Kindergarten

People live to please themselves. I did that for many years. It was true in the days of Ruth and it's still true today. I went on a rabbit trail yesterday and as I was reading the book of Ruth, the Lord brought to my memory a poster that once hung on my wall in my little room on Orleans Drive – Everything I Need to Know I Learned in Kindergarten.

Ruth was a Moabite, from a nation formed out of a desperate incestuous relationship between Lot and his daughter. They were a depraved generation, completely antagonistic, arrogant, stubborn, and rebellious. They lacked impulse control; yet, one woman followed the still small voice of a God she had only heard about and she kept it simple. Out of her obedience came the easy concepts that should drive us all today. Life doesn't have to be so hard.

Ruth had married into a Jewish family and all the men had tragically died leaving behind her Jewish mother-in-law, her sister-in-law, and herself. God's grace is sufficient. He offers it in the middle of difficult circumstances.

Ruth 1:3-5 – Now Elimelek, Naomi's husband, died, and she was left with her two sons. 4 They married Moabite women, one named Orpah and the other Ruth. After they had lived there about ten years, 5 both Mahlon and Kilion also died, and Naomi was left without her two sons and her husband.

Rule #1 – Goldfish, hamsters, and even the little white seed in the Styrofoam cup – they all die. So do we.

Death is inevitable. It's how we react to it that shows our true character. Naomi allowed it to make her bitter.

Ruth 1:20-21 - "Don't call me Naomi," she told them. "Call me Mara, because the Almighty has made my life very bitter. 21 I went away full, but the Lord has brought me back empty. Why call me Naomi? The Lord has afflicted me; the Almighty has brought misfortune upon me."

This doesn't just apply to the natural death of a body, but we can also become bitter to the death of dreams, relationships, and even our own spirits. Life can make us bitter or better, pitiful or powerful. In Naomi's "Woe is me" sate, she begged her daughters-in-law to go away, to leave her alone, to go on with their young lives, but Ruth decided to stick out the bitterness and God blessed her with His perfect example of impartiality.

Ruth 1:16-18 – But Ruth replied, "Don't urge me to leave you or to turn back from you. Where you go I will go, and where you stay I will stay. Your people will be my people and your God my God. 17 Where you die I will die, and there I will be buried. May the Lord deal with me, be it ever so severely, if anything but death separates you and me." 18 When Naomi realized that Ruth was determined to go with her, she stopped urging her.

Rule #2 – When you go out into the world, watch out of traffic, hold hands, and stick together.

They arrived in Bethlehem, Naomi's home, and Ruth was put to work while Naomi continued to grieve, having forgotten that Ruth's husband had also died. The fields of Boaz had leftover grain saved for orphans and widow, and in humility, she gleaned what was appropriate and the good Lord provided and also showed her favor.

Rule #3 – Don't take things that aren't yours.

Ruth 2:15-18 - As she got up to glean, Boaz gave orders to his men, "Let her gather among the sheaves and don't reprimand her. 16 Even pull out some stalks for her from the bundles and leave them for her to pick up, and don't rebuke her." 17 So Ruth gleaned in the field until evening. Then she threshed the barley she had gathered, and it amounted to about an ephah. 18 She carried it back to town, and her mother-in-law saw how much she had gathered. Ruth also brought out and gave her what she had left over after she had eaten enough.

Rule #4 – Share everything.

She could have left with her provisions but she worked until evening anyway. Boaz had already given her enough, but she worked for it anyway. Nothing irks me more than people who take and take and take and never give back. Naomi's spirits went from nagging and complaining to joy and adulation overnight and a plan was formed for redemption. Hope glimmered on the horizon. Naomi's wheels began to spin and she realized she had to get up and do something or her and Ruth would die widows.

Rule #5 – Clean up your own mess.

It was a new day to make things right in the eyes of God and man and Ruth rolled with it.

Ruth 3:5-6 - "I will do whatever you say," Ruth answered. 6 So she went down to the threshing floor and did everything her mother-in-law told her to do.

Rule #6 – Be willing to listen to the advice of those older than you. Their knowledge is invaluable.

Because of Ruth's obedience, Boaz agreed to redeem her, marry her, and give her children...that is, if another man didn't step to the plate first.

Ruth 3:9-14 - "Who are you?" he asked. "I am your servant Ruth," she said. "Spread the corner of your garment over me, since you are a guardian-redeemer of our family." 10 "The Lord bless you, my daughter," he replied. "This kindness is greater than that which you showed earlier: You have not run after the younger men, whether rich or poor. 11 And now, my daughter, don't be afraid. I will do for you all you ask. All the people of my town know that you are a woman of noble character. 12 Although it is true that I am a guardian-redeemer of our family, there is another who is more closely related than I. 13 Stay here for the night, and in the morning if he wants to do his duty as your guardian-redeemer, good; let him redeem you. But if he is not willing, as surely as the Lord lives I will do it. Lie here until morning." 14 So she lay at his feet until morning, but got up before anyone could be recognized; and he said, "No one must know that a woman came to the threshing floor."

He put her back in a place where her character wouldn't be questioned.

Rule #7 – Put things back where you found them.

When the time for redemption came, every heart that beat in the circumstance fluttered at the mere promise of what was to come, but it had to play out keeping everyone's character in balance.

Ruth 4:4-6 - I thought I should bring the matter to your attention and suggest that you buy it in the presence of these seated here and in the presence of the elders of my people. If you will redeem it, do so. But if you will not, tell me, so I will know. For no one has the right to do it except you, and I am next in line." "I will redeem it," he said. 5 Then Boaz said, "On the day you buy the land from Naomi, you also acquire Ruth the Moabite, the dead man's widow, in order to maintain the name of the dead with his property." 6 At this, the guardian-redeemer said, "Then I cannot redeem it because I might endanger my own estate. You redeem it yourself. I cannot do it."

Rule #8 – Play fair.

The thing is, I don't have to think so hard and I don't have to take shortcuts. Even in my depths of despair, God can bring forth blessings. He shows me glimpses of the promises, not to have me in overdrive thinking mode about how I am going to get there, but to show me there is a hope and a reason to keep going. All I have to do is continue to step out in willing obedience and look for Him in every situation.

Rule #9 – And then remember the Dick and Jane books and the first word you learned – the biggest word of all – LOOK.

Look to the word of God for understanding and for proof that even when there seems to be no way, He can make a way, and He ALWAYS gets His way. Boaz was a descendant of the only family of survivors in the siege of Jericho, he was born from the line of Rahab, a prostitute. Ruth was a foreigner from a pagan nation. They became the parents of Obed.

Ruth 4:22 – Obed the father of Jesse, and Jesse the father of David.

Out of this direct line came our Messiah. Don't over think. Keep it simple. And follow the rules.

79 – Grain of Sand

"All it was meant to be was a grain of sand"...those are the words I woke up to in my spirit when I was napping yesterday. Quickly, almost instantaneously, the Lord spoke into my spirit the moments in my life that He was referring to and they flashed before my very eyes as I opened them to the world out of my deep sleep. I grabbed a pen and piece of paper and this is what came out of the revelation He was bestowing on me as I was still wiping the sleep from my eyes:

"I had a dream. The Hand of God was before me and I looked upon it with interest as He scooped up from the seashore a colossal amount of sand into His large hand. The sand represented my life and each grain was a moment of my life passing by as it slipped through His hand, one by one, each grain of sand slowly and peacefully flowing through the fingers of His Mighty Hand. I took a grain of the sand and put it into the mouth of an oyster and willed it with all my might to become a pearl. I wanted it to be beautiful. I desired for it to grow. I wanted that moment to last a bit longer and tarry in the Hand of God, lasting longer than the other grains of sand. As the one grain stayed in the oyster, other moments were passing me by as they slipped unnoticed through the hand of God and I missed them because I was focused on the oyster and not on the grains of sand slowing passing through His hand. My attention was diverted from God and the oyster became my obsession. Meanwhile, while I wasn't looking, God had taken His own oyster, and deposited into it His own grain of sand and it grew into a beautiful pearl but I wasn't paying attention. By this time I was frustrated and more moments were passing me by because time doesn't stand still for God and the sand continued to flow through His hand. I opened my oyster and found nothing but a grain of sand. I couldn't will for it to become a pearl, so I chose to put it back into the hand of God and it passed through, just another moment of my life and for a moment I was saddened but not for long. You see? That grain of sand was not God's best for me, it was never intended to be a pearl, it was only meant to be a grain of sand."

Why do we take moments in our lives and force our will upon them when His best for us has already been prepared? How many grains of sand pass through time in His hand while we are being impatient with the one grain we chose for ourselves? When will we see that He alone can move time and space to put the right grain of sand into the right oyster and it isn't random at all to Him? The pearls of our lives will stay in His hand for eternity as the rest of our lives pass us by, but only the ones HE chooses for us. So many times I have tried to make pearls when it was only meant to be a grain of sand. He has already prepared the most exquisite, beautiful pearl that will last into eternity.

This revelation was huge for me in this moment in my life, in the smack dab middle of this messy divorce. I'm free today, even more so today than I was yesterday, to seek His pearls for my life. The rest, I am letting go of and I am allowing it slip through His fingers, as it should have all along. It was only meant to be a grain of sand.

Matthew 13:45-46 (NIV) - 45 "Again, the kingdom of heaven is like a merchant looking for fine pearls.46 When he found one of great value, he went away and sold everything he had and bought it."

EIGHTY – *Good Morning Sunshine*

Good Morning Sunshine! Where have you been? I have been waiting expectantly for you to arrive. I haven't seen you in some time. You are always looking, but never really seeking. Why won't you see Me? I am the beautiful aroma in your coffee. I am the emerald green in the grass that sparkles with the freshness of the dew. As you ponder stepping on it trying to imagine what it must feel like, I am the wind that against your face.

Do you hear them? It's the birds as they open their eyes to a new and fresh morning. I provide for them and they lack nothing, so what makes you think I can't provide for you? They are singing to Me a sweet song that I wrote for them upon their creation. Isn't it beautiful? I am the breeze in the trees and the hum through the branches. I am the sleep in your eye as you wipe away your tears upon remembering the nightmare you had last night. I held you as you wept but you did not know.

I am the light that comes from the morning sun as it peeks over the horizon in a slow and steady way as to not wake everyone else too soon. I am like an eager puppy, bouncing from place to place ahead of you just hoping that you will catch My eye and flash Me one smile. As you move from room to room not sure of yourself this morning and the day that lies ahead, know that I have already gone there and I am waiting patiently with open arms knowing that all you need right now is to fall into them. I am in every single breath that you take. I am the warmth in the bed that is calling you to get back in it. Please don't do that. Spend this time with Me. My heart breaks because I long for you.

When I hear your alarm go off and you choose to hit the snooze button I am downcast because that could have been precious time with Me. I know where you are going and I know where you have been and I am with you. Everything is going to be ok. Don't be anxious today. Cast all your worries on Me.

Don't get so busy this morning seeing what someone did only hours ago on social media. Cuddle on the floor with Me and just rest for a while. You don't have to say much, other that you love Me. That is all I need to hear. I am desperate for you. No one on earth can compare to you. The coffee is ready. I know how you like it; two spoonfuls of sugar and lots of cream. Would you like Me to read to you? All you have to do is open the Book in front of you. It has all the answers to all the questions that you could EVER ask about life. You have the keys to freedom right there in the palm of your hand. You are more precious to Me than gold and any jewel in the world. Come sit a spell, lean against Me, and allow Me to show you WHO I AM.

Psalm 5:3 – In the morning, Lord, you hear my voice; in the morning I lay my requests before you and wait expectantly.

81 – *The Valley*

The valley is beautiful. I feel like someone needs to be reminded of that. Why do we put such awful expectations on what the valley that we are being drug through looks like? The Word of the Lord says that we will go from strength to strength and glory to glory as we pass through our Valley of Weeping, but who is to say that our tears aren't watering the flowers and making them grow?

Psalm 84:5-9 (NIV) - Blessed are those whose strength is in you, whose hearts are set on pilgrimage. 6 As they pass through the Valley of Baka, they make it a place of springs; the autumn rains also cover it with pools. 7 They go from strength to strength, till each appears before God in Zion. 8 Hear my prayer, Lord God Almighty; listen to me, God of Jacob. 9 Look on our shield, O God; look with favor on your anointed one.

Even though we think of the mountain as our pinnacle, our time of arrival, our destination, the air is still very thin and cannot sustain us for long. We are silly to think that we can live up there without perishing. The valley is inevitable, but it is what you make it. What does your valley look like? Is it scattered with debris of the past? Does it haunt you at night with ghosts of what should have been? Do the barren rocks cause you to stumble as you grope around through the dirt? Are you eyes temporarily blinded by past hurts and regrets? What do you see below? Has God lifted you high above the clouds to really look at a wasteland? Or has He brought you to the mountain top to see and perceive the TRUTH? What if what you see through your tinted glasses is fertile land ready for a harvest? What if all it is, is a place to travel through on your way to a new and improved destination? What is your perception? The valley only looks as good or as bad as YOU perceive it.

Ezekiel 36:8-11 (NIV) - But you, mountains of Israel, will produce branches and fruit for my people Israel, for they will soon come home. 9 I am concerned for you and will look on you with favor; you will be plowed and sown, 10 and I will cause many people to live on you—yes, all of Israel. The towns will be inhabited and the ruins rebuilt. 11 I will increase the number of people and animals living on you, and they will be fruitful and become numerous. I will settle people on you as in the past and will make you prosper more than before. Then you will know that I am the Lord.

Have you ever driven past a beautiful meadow, partaken of its delicate array of flowers, desired to sit or lie down on its thick, lush green grass? Have you ever reflected on that meadow where the birds sing songs to the Creator and the small wildlife frolic in the distance? Have you ever driven past it again, only to be appalled at the sight of that same meadow, completely torn up and in ruins? The farmer has come and dug up all that was beautiful and the rocks and soil replace the once green grass. What do you perceive NOW? Do you see the eventual abundant harvest, or do you just see the sadness of what used to be? It's really just a choice. Some of us can't see the harvest because we fear the unknown.

***Genesis 15:1 (NIV) - After this, the word of
the Lord came to Abram in a vision: "Do not be
afraid, Abram. I am your shield, your very great
reward."***

You are protected - on the mountain top AND in the
valley. Even where there seems to be no way and we are
begging for new eyes to see the truth of what is around
us instead of the devastation, He will show us the
promise. Even when your eyes are clouded with tears,
the valley and all its beauty is being washed by the
water and the blood. See it for what it really is and not
what it should be and everything will be right with your
soul.

82 – *Humble Pie*

I had a girl at Jacob's Well Recovery Center for Women ask me recently what it was like to have to come back into the program a second time after my near fatal relapse.

This is what I said, "Do you remember making mud pies as a kid and no matter how bad it tasted, you were going to eat it anyway only because of the pride you had and the effort it took in making it?"
Her reply, "Absolutely!"
I stated, "Humble pie tastes a lot like a mud pie. It is grainy, it goes down gritty, is tasteless, and no amount of pretending can turn it into a delicious chocolate dream. However, I had to eat it because I made that pie when I chose to do what I did to lead me back into these chairs. I had to come back and profess to know nothing, even though I thought I knew everything."

Psalm 119:71-72 (NIV) - It was good for me to be afflicted so that I might learn your decrees. 72 The law from your mouth is more precious to me than thousands of pieces of silver and gold.

No one wants to admit when they are wrong (well...maybe some people do...I still struggle). I seem to always need to have the last word and in all honesty I cannot stand to be corrected or rebuked for behavior that I thought was completely necessary in the moment. But it's absolutely paramount for me to shut my big mouth and listen to godly counsel when things are obviously chaotic and confusing due to my own compromises. I listen to my own voice as it is raised in defense and wonder who I even am and then I wonder if the person on the receiving end is fed up enough with me yet to just walk on out. Pride and arrogance are not my friends.

Philippians 2:3-4 (NIV) - Do nothing out of selfish ambition or vain conceit. Rather, in humility value others above yourselves, 4 not looking to your own interests but each of you to the interests of the others.

I am so very grateful for the people in my life who stand on the watchtower and warn me when I am becoming too full of myself - those who point out the pitfalls before I step in and make camp - the chosen few who don't put up with my crap when I am throwing it every which way but up. Newsflash: I do not know everything! I thank God for making me new, clothing me in peace, hemming me in on all sides so that even on days when I forget who He says I am and revert back to my old ways, I can look up and know that He sustains me.

83 – *What is Normal?*

What is normal? I've been on a pretty even keel lately, as if the waves of uncertainty that crash around me have finally settled down for just a moment and are merely lapping at the side of my boat with the gentle breeze blowing in the wind. Is this what normal feels like?

I'm so used to the storms of life that take me under and into the great deep unknown. I always desired to be normal but I never felt like it was attainable. I always knew I was different but I strongly desired to be like everyone else. That caused me to hate myself even more when I didn't feel like I could keep up with the Jones' and it became another excuse to check out of my painful existence and dive deeper into the realms of darkness. My definition of normal changed with the tide. It was always dependent on who I was around and what THEIR definition was.

Webster defines "Normal" as usual or ordinary; not strange; mentally and physically healthy. Wow! That doesn't define me at ALL! As a follower of Christ, I am called to stand out, not to fit into a mold that society created. Sure, the white picket fence and cute little dog and 2.5 kids sounds great, but isn't that what everyone *else* says will make me happy? Why?

Romans 12:2 (NIV) - Do not conform to the pattern of this world, but be transformed by the renewing of your mind. Then you will be able to test and approve what God's will is—his good, pleasing and perfect will.

I am so used to extremes, that being still and patient and ok with all that is surrounding me and coming against me is not MY normal. Each day for me is beginning to take on a new wonder of generality and it's beautiful! I'm creating and defining a new "normal" and I don't care what anyone else has to say about what that looks like. I'm at peace. Why fit in when I can stand out? I may be worn out from this journey, falling into my bed each night exhausted from the trip. I may be weary, but it means I have made a difference. I may be mentally challenged every single day to the point of feeling insane because of the attack of the enemy, but I can rest in the presence of God and know who HE says I am. I am NOT normal, nor do I desire to be. The basis of my self-worth is my identity in Christ, not man.

Proverbs 30:25 (NIV) - she is clothed with strength and dignity; she can laugh at the days to come.

84 – *Self-Vindication*

Ridiculed? Slandered? Talked about? Despised? Misrepresented? Ignored? Felt like you didn't exist? Welcome to the party. Now is NOT the time for self-vindication.

Sometimes I feel like I have suffered a cruel blow to my ego. Nothing compares to the lonely feelings of rejection, especially when it seems to be coming from people I love and respect. My flesh desperately cries out for revenge. Don't they see the injustice? Doesn't anyone understand what I am going through?

In moments like these I can CHOOSE to let it take me out, or I can look upon myself and my ways for clues to the reason behind the madness in the first place. I can make the choice to stay in my head and let "paranoia" reign free, or I can follow the example of Christ and forgive myself for my own shortcomings which caused the discord and in turn forgive my accusers.

It's not up to me to change the hearts of people. No one person on the planet should have power over me or my thoughts unless I give it to them.

Mark 15:5 – But Jesus made no reply, and Pilate was amazed.

There He stands, the ultimate example of self-assurance and peace which no one else could ever imitate. What is stopping me from completing the work that this Man called me do on earth?

Mark 14:60-61 - Then the high priest stood up before them and asked Jesus, are you not going to answer? What is this testimony that these men are bringing against you?" 61 But Jesus remained silent and gave no answer. Again the high priest asked him, "Are you the Messiah, the Son of the Blessed One?"

You know, sometimes the evidence against me is overwhelming and in order to be set free I must tell the truth. Sometimes the accusations are merely fabricated. It's times like those when it is best just to remain silent before those who revile me. Regardless, it is ALL painful – but there is pain in the offering. God sees and knows everything.

1 Corinthians 4:10-20 (MSG) - 9-13 It seems to me that God has put us who bear his Message on stage in a theater in which no one wants to buy a ticket. We're something everyone stands around and stares at, like an accident in the street. We're the Messiah's misfits. You might be sure of yourselves, but we live in the midst of frailties and uncertainties. You might be well-thought-of by others, but we're mostly kicked around. Much of the time we don't have enough to eat, we wear patched and threadbare clothes, we get doors slammed in our faces, and we pick up odd jobs anywhere we can to eke out a living. When they call us names, we say, "God bless you." When they spread rumors about us, we put in a good word for them. We're treated like garbage, potato peelings from the culture's kitchen. And it's not getting any better.

14-16 I'm not writing all this as a neighborhood scold just to make you feel rotten. I'm writing as a father to you, my children. I love you and want you to grow up well, not spoiled. There are a lot of people around who can't wait to tell you what you've done wrong, but there aren't many fathers willing to take the time and effort to help you grow up. It was as Jesus helped me proclaim God's Message to you that I became your father. I'm not, you know, asking you to do anything I'm not already doing myself.

17 This is why I sent Timothy to you earlier. He is also my dear son, and true to the Master. He will refresh your memory on the instructions I regularly give all the churches on the way of Christ.

18-20 I know there are some among you who are so full of themselves they never listen to anyone, let alone me. They don't think I'll ever show up in person. But I'll be there sooner than you think, God willing, and then we'll see if they're full of anything but hot air. God's Way is not a matter of mere talk; it's an empowered life.

85 – *Avoid Regret*

"Avoid Regret...Avoid Impaired Driving", said the sign on the highway to Memphis on a beautiful, sunny afternoon recently. Immediately I began to ponder the application God gave me with these few simple words.

2 Corinthians 7:10 (ESV) – For godly grief produces a repentance that leads to salvation without regret, whereas worldly grief produces death.

For so very long I thrived on "Regret". "Regret" was my long lost friend who went with me on one journey after another, always the back seat driver that told me where to go, how to drive, where to turn, when to slow down, which turn to take. "Regret" always whispered in my ear reminding me always of the place from which I had just come. "Regret" was the still, small voice that told me all about myself and kept me in the "woe is me" mentality. I would pick up that lonely hitchhiker when things became too hard, when life would just show up, when my insecurities would overshadow the good things in my life. My mom always told me not to pick up hitchhikers on the side of the road, strangers looking for a ride to nowhere but somewhere.

The problem was, picking up "Regret" was easy, because "Regret" wasn't a stranger to me. It was another excuse I used to continue driving on my road to insanity.

Isaiah 43:18-19 (ESV) - "Remember not the former things, nor consider the things of old. Behold, I am doing a new thing; now it springs forth, do you not perceive it? I will make a way in the wilderness and rivers in the desert."

How many times do we hold onto "Regret", choosing to pick it up and keep in our car so we can feel sorry for ourselves and get others to co-sign our craziness? Who is really driving the car we are in? Are we driving, impaired by "Regret"? Or have we let Jesus take the wheel? Who is really driving us to our future? It's time to put "Regret" back on the road to nowhere and leave it behind. However, here is a warning... "Objects in mirror are closer than they appear", so don't turn around to pick it back up. It's a trick of the eyes and the heart. Put "Regret" on the highway with its baggage that is too heavy for you to carry and move on. Look out the front window and don't look back.

Proverbs 4:25-27 (NIV) – Olet your eyes look straight ahead; fix your gaze directly before you. 26 Give careful thought to the paths for your feet and be steadfast in all your ways. 27 Do not turn to the right or the left; keep your foot from evil.

86 — Faith and Belief

Faith and Belief were sent out on a mission like no other. To the human eye they were smaller than the stars in the night sky as the floated carelessly down from heaven toward the new baby who was soon to be born into the world. Their size didn't matter after all, God had told them, because all He needed was for them to always keep their new charge following the Light of Truth. That seemed simple enough, considering this baby was just announced in heaven to the angelic host as the Lord called out her name with love and excitement. Her name was "Victory"!

She was just there in heaven with them and she herself had been sent on a very important mission. As they took over their newest responsibility and cared for her with love and compassion, teaching her from a very young age to trust and obey and always believe in the One who sent her, life at first was good. There was love, joy, peace, forbearance, kindness, goodness, faithfulness, gentleness, and self-control!

Then it happened, some unexpected heartache that threatened the very existence of the human girl. Her spirit had been broken and crushed and in came wave after wave of Fear, Doubt, and Uncertainty. Faith and Belief were then sent AWAY by CHOICE?!?!? "She has a CHOICE? We didn't know this was possible!!", they asked themselves as they watched from afar as the Light of Truth grew ever so dim. "What are we to do now? She doesn't even know we are still here!!"

Faith then followed Reason into uncharted territory just to have something of the girl to hold onto. Belief was lost to the darkness and Faith was so sad without that companion.

Time seemed to stand still as both from their own vantage points watched as the girl chose despair and darkness over Truth and Light, seemingly against her very own will. "But we KNOW her purpose!" they screamed. "WE HEARD GOD AND WE KNOW HER PROMISE!", but it was to no avail.

There was nothing Faith and Belief could do without the girl choosing a new path, and the Light of Truth was almost now non-existent. They watched and they waited for the open door, and not as patiently as they should have. People came and people went who tried to share the Light of Truth with the girl but nothing worked. Then a miracle!! The brokenness of the girl was more than she could even bear, and there was no other choice but to surrender.

The Lord saw fit from His Throne to rebuke the enemy and said, "Enough already! She is broken enough. Now I can use her for her purpose. Leave her be!" He then set in motion a chain of events that led the girl directly to the right people at the right place at the right time and life for her was never the same. Faith left Reason and flooded the girl's new and improved heart and Belief was finally set free from captivity! The reunion was more than they could handle as they witnessed the Light of Truth grow increasingly brighter and brighter by the day! Her purpose is now being fulfilled.

Persecution, heartache, and sadness still come; but, today they accomplish a new objective, to find others like her and bring them closer to the Light of Truth.

Who are you helping along your journey to find that Light? Have you found it and are just holding onto it? Or are you TRULY showing it to others, even those you don't care to be seen with lest you be ridiculed or mocked? God is for EVERYONE and we all have the same Holy Spirit. NO ONE is better than, more spiritual than.

No one has a higher calling than, or has the right to look down and frown upon anyone and their own walk. We are all sent here as guides, to love and respect those others who are just walking out their salvation with fear and trembling before the Lord. Don't turn your back. We all experience heartache and rejection, but that is not an excuse. Are you shining the Light of Truth? Or are you pushing others back into the dark?

Matthew 25:40 - 40 "The King will reply, 'Truly I tell you, whatever you did for one of the least of these brothers and sisters of mine, you did for me.' Matthew 25:45 - 45 "He will reply, 'Truly I tell you, whatever you did not do for one of the least of these, you did not do for me.'

87 – Resist

1 Peter 5:6-9 - Humble yourselves, therefore, under God's mighty hand, that he may lift you up in due time. 7 Cast all your anxiety on him because he cares for you. 8 Be alert and of sober mind. Your enemy the devil prowls around like a roaring lion looking for someone to devour. 9 Resist him, standing firm in the faith, because you know that the family of believers throughout the world is undergoing the same kind of sufferings.

I was thinking last night as I fell into a deep sleep about nature. I am moved by creation itself and my mind sometimes has difficulty comprehending how the earth and everything on it just ebbs and flows. Life flourishes in many forms, from the algae on a pond to our highest level of existence and intelligence - a human.

Nature itself completes a revolution in the circle of life every day.

Imagine being a gazelle, wandering the African plains under a hot sun. There is no fear, only joy and peace as you bound through the tall grass alongside your family toward water. You have no worries, no anxious thoughts as you meander through the world on a course for mere survival. Nothing of the world causes you to question the divine creation in which you live, but you find yourself cautious and alert.

In the tall grass, just beyond your view, lies a predator in wait. He is patiently seeking his next meal, overcome by a fierce hunger. The lion's watchful eyes scan the horizon as thousands of your kind leap through the air in joyful rhythm and praise to their Creator unseen. He is looking, as he prowls the plains, for a weakling that he can pounce upon. However, God sees and God protects the weak and the lost.

So, little gazelle, stand fast and flee temptation. Don't stop to gaze upon the lion with peaked curiosity. Be determined to reach the water which will cleanse you and keep you safe. Guard your heart, remain humble, lower yourself and your thinking, and admit your need for holy and eternal deliverance. When you are weak, God is strong! He will lift you up and set your feet on solid ground!

88 – *Circle of Life*

I wrote this for one of the strongest women I know upon her graduation from Jacob's Well this past Sunday. This was her second time at Jacob's Well, as it was mine. The battle is very real and some of us get wounded and need time for healing before heading back out into the evil and perverse world.

She prayed her daughter back into Jacob's Well and her beautiful child walked across the threshold angry, hurt, and confused. The daughter is also at Jacob's Well for a second time. Watching my friend reverently pray for her daughter, powerless but not without hope, was the most awe inspiring things I have ever seen. To see the prayer answered and generational curses being broken before my very eyes is a testament to God's mercy and grace. Happy Graduation, dear friend! I was honored to hand you your certificate of graduation! Thank you for reminding me why I do what I do:

"Friend, you asked me a long time ago to write something for you and your beautiful daughter before your graduation and you are probably assuming that I forgot. Well, I didn't. As I sat with my own mother in a small, intimate booth at a restaurant this weekend, I had time to reflect. I could feel her presence next to me and I craved it long before she even uttered the word "goodbye" to me again. I held her hand and watched her tears as we spoke of my own children who we both have yet to see in quite some time.

What I realized in that moment is that a mother's love is like a circle, it has no beginning and no end. Her love for me is the same I feel toward my own children and the same I will feel toward their children one day, even though we are miles apart. It is the same love you feel toward your daughter, her children, and the child she is now carrying. It has no end. We allow ourselves to be bound by the mistakes of the past and the circle then changes drastically. One regret leads to another bad decision out of guilt and the next thing you know we are trapped inside of the circle that was once ringed with nothing but love but that is now tainted with the shame of the past. HOWEVER, that circle can be broken and another one completely built that centers around Christ. The spiral of death can be changed again into the circle of life, with one decision based on a solid commitment to put Christ alone at the center of it all.

My own mother told me this weekend that she felt guilty for her own behaviors that eventually led to the kink in which I was able to slip through unnoticed, out of the circle of love, into the spiral of rejection, abandonment, and fear. It's the same guilt I feel about the destruction of my own family and the estrangement of my own children. However, in my mother's own prayer, as she pushed aside her private regret, angels heard her sorrow and ministered to me in my deepest pit of hell, because of the LOVE.

It's what I see in you and your daughter. You both came into this program, you fought for both of your lives, you both fell, the circle was broken, the trust was gone, the co-dependency ran rampant, but the LOVE still remained. It's the same LOVE that Christ has for all of us.

1 Corinthians 13:13 – And now these three remain: faith, hope, and love. But the greatest of these is love.

You had faith, you held out hope, and you loved until your heart was bleeding. My mother loved me back to life until Christ could do surgery on my heart, and you loved your child right back over the threshold of Jacob's Well, until Christ could mend both of you together. The enemy wants you both dead, because together you are a fighting force for God that cannot be stopped. You have a mission that far exceeds anything the world could ever comprehend. Together, you will change lives, see families healed, testify to the saving and transforming power of Christ that can sweep through the generations before and the generations past and put circles back together that should have remained broken forever and into eternity.

Isaiah 43:1-7 (NIV) - "Do not fear, for I have redeemed you; I have summoned you by name; you are mine. 2 When you pass through the waters, I will be with you; and when you pass through the rivers, they will not sweep over you. When you walk through the fire, you will not be burned; the flames will not set you ablaze. 3 For I am the Lord your God, the Holy One of Israel, your Savior; I give Egypt for your ransom, Cush and Seba in your stead. 4 Since you are precious and honored in my sight, and because I love you, I will give people in exchange for you, nations in exchange for your life. 5 Do not be afraid, for I am with you; I will bring your children from the east and gather you from the west. 6 I will say to the north, 'Give them up!' and to the south, 'Do not hold them back.' Bring my sons from afar and my daughters from the ends of the earth – 7 everyone who is called by my name, whom I created for my glory, whom I formed and made."

This is a charge to you and a promise if you obey. Don't allow the circumstances of life to sway you from making godly decisions, even if you feel as if you are drowning. The life raft is there, a circle thrown in the storm to save you from yourself. Lisa, you chose to put the oxygen mask on first, then you passed it to your dying child before the fire consumed the whole plane. Because of that decision, you both sit here today. I am so proud of you, I am honored to call you my sister and friend, and I can't wait to see God move in you both to bring others back into the circle of life and love."

89 – *Truth*

John 8:32 – You will know the truth, and the truth will set you free.

Recently, while reading in Numbers, I came across a section that reminded me so much of the struggle that is faced every single day by the women of Jacob's Well Ministries and Recovery Center. It is a battle, to say the least, to continue to stand when the giants in life seem so daunting compared to the allure of the Promised Land which is right on the horizon. The land itself is so incredibly beautiful, yet so many of the women sabotage it and listen to the bad reports coming from the scouts on the battlefield instead of listening to the Spirit of God. They choose to go back to the wilderness.

Numbers 13:27-28 (NIV) – The gave Moses this account: "We went into the land to which you sent us, and it does flow with milk and honey! Here is its fruit. 28 But the people who live there are powerful, and the cities are fortified and very large."

So many women walk across the threshold and see the fruit immediately. They see the promise as if it has already happened, then come the reports, then a few bad decisions, and the next thing you know, they are back out the and back on the wrong side of the battlefield.

Numbers 14:1-4 (NIV) – That night all the members of the community raised their voices and wept aloud. 2 All the Israelites grumbled against Moses and Aaron, and the whole assembly said to them, "If only we had died in Egypt! Or in this wilderness! 3 Why is the Lord bringing us to this land only to

let us fall by the sword? Our wives and children will be taken as plunder. Wouldn't it be better for us to go back to Egypt?" 4 And they said to each other, "We should choose a leader and go back to Egypt."

There is a woman at Jacob's Well as I type this who did just that. She listened to the wrong report, made a decision that cost her, and fled out the and back into the waiting arms of the enemy. She refused to cut the head off her giant that stood in the way of her Promised Land and she was gone in an instant. This was last year. After racking up five felony charges, countless rapes, a beating and pistol whipping which left her nearly dead, and a lifetime of regret, shame and guilt, she graced the threshold of Jacob's Well once again, barely breathing, not able to hold her head up for one second. She had chosen to go back to Egypt, as many do on a weekly basis, and it cost her more oil in her alabaster jar. Here is what she wrote as she made a conscious decision to face the giants in her life head on. Needless to say, the enemy is mad, and he has lost his power over her life that she is reclaiming through Christ!

"I do what I want to do because I want to do it. I don't work hard because I don't want to. I don't care to talk about what I want. If I want to talk about someone in the program, I do because it's what I want to do. It's always about what I want to do. I want people to like me because it gets me what I want, so I become whoever they want me to be in order to acquire their approval. I act like their friend and let them confide in me then the moment I see an opportunity for personal gain I turn on them. I know weaknesses when I see them in people and I use it to my advantage. I know that in their desire to have a friend in me that I can get them to let me

get away with whatever I want and that I can get what I want from them. Everything I do is for personal gain and I'll take from whomever and whatever stands in between me and what I want. I do not submit to authority and I'm not open to receive your advice. The evil I am capable of is inconceivable. I got manipulation down to a science and can use it to get just about whatever I want from pretty much whoever I want. There is so much darkness in me that I barely have any remorse for my actions and almost no empathy for others. For a long time I lied to myself by thinking I was a very good person and blaming everyone else for every bad decision I made. Now I'm blown away by the truth and I realize now that what I've been hiding is that I actually hate myself. I've finally realized the truth and you can't change what you don't acknowledge. Now that I see this, I am going to change. I don't want to stay on the path to self destruction or drag others down with me."

That, folks, is deliverance!! That is truth and truth is costly. Truth means war!! She did something afraid and that is now propelling her past the popular opinion of the world and into doing what God has called her to do. She is no longer following the path of practicality, but is listening to and obeying God, no longer wandering in an aimless and fruitless desert. She is recalling God's glorious promises and no longer slipping into doubt! Christ alone is setting her free!

Romans 7:14-25 (NIV) - We know that the law is spiritual; but I am unspiritual, sold as a slave to sin. 15 I do not understand what I do. For what I want to do I do not do, but what I hate I do. 16 And if I do what I do not want to do, I agree that the law is good. 17 As it is, it is no longer I myself who do it, but it is sin living in me. 18 For I know that good itself does not dwell in me, that is, in my sinful nature. For I have the desire to do what is good, but I cannot carry it out. 19 For I do not do the good I want to do, but the evil I do not want to do—this I keep on doing.20 Now if I do what I do not want to do, it is no longer I who do it, but it is sin living in me that does it. 21 So I find this law at work: Although I want to do good, evil is right there with me. 22 For in my inner being I delight in God's law; 23 but I see another law at work in me, waging war against the law of my mind and making me a prisoner of the law of sin at work within me. 24 What a wretched man I am! Who will rescue me from this body that is subject to death? 25 Thanks be to God, who delivers me through Jesus Christ our Lord!

What truth are you refusing to see? How raw are YOU willing to get? How long are you going to stay in the desert listening to bad reports and begging to go back to your oppression? Get real, get honest before the Lord, and allow Him to do a mighty work in transforming your mind!

90 – Center of the Tornado

There is a brewing storm outside. The sky becomes very dark and ominous as the firmament is filled quickly with the fullness of foreboding black clouds. The wind picks up its pace as if it knows what is to come and is running from it. As it blows through the trees, leaves are scattered unwillingly along the ground, around and around in circles, ripped from their places of rest. The rain comes now in sheets, watering the grass and bringing much needed life to vegetation. The clouds above grow darker and the sky turns a green haze. There it is. The tornado is snaking out of the sky, looming overhead as its single tentacle reaches from the heavens toward the ground, threatening to destroy everything in its path. There is nowhere to turn to escape. I close my eyes and expect to be swept away. As it gets closer, the rain stops and there is a calm before this storm. I know now not to get complacent or excited in that calm, still air. It doesn't mean the storm isn't still ahead. As I stand in the path of this giant fore, I wonder where it is going to sweep me off to. Is it going to destroy me? Maime me? Kill me? I brace myself for the wind that will change me as its swirling mass of huge, leftover debris and wind come upon me. This is the end. But WAIT! I open my eyes. Where am I? The winds of change are all around me. I can see as I turn in a circle the debris of chaos, confusion, rejection, fear, hopelessness, abandonment, doubt, and insecurity all around me. The winds are blowing, but I am safe in the center of the storm.

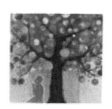# Epilogue

God is not on the pages in the book of Esther, nor was He on the pages of my book for a very long time. It doesn't mean He wasn't there, producing and directing a show, setting me in places I never thought I would be.

Esther was the most unlikely candidate for Queen. She was the wrong nationality, and she even had to hide her true identity, but she was called to save a nation from annihilation and she had FAVOR. Esther becoming Queen was nearly impossible, just like my situation looks impossible, but God lavishes in the impossible because He then gets all the glory. He uses me now, not because of me, but in spite of me.

I was afforded and extended not one, but two - 6 month opportunities at Jacob's Well, a full 12 months of purification at the hands of beautiful men and women of God who cared for me and taught me how to hear my own name.

Esther 2:12-14 - Before a young woman's turn came to go in to King Xerxes, she had to complete twelve months of beauty treatments prescribed for the women, six months with oil of myrrh and six with perfumes and cosmetics. 13 And this is how she would go to the king: Anything she wanted was given her to take with her from the harem to the king's palace. 14 In the evening she would go there and in the morning return to another part of the harem to the care of Shaashgaz, the king's eunuch who was in charge of the concubines. She would not return to the king unless he was pleased with her and summoned her by name.

I fell short and was not qualified to go where God is leading me, but I was called anyway. The names of the past that I answered to on a daily basis still ring in my ear; however, today I hear God calling my name and His voice overshadows the rest and resounds in my heart and spirit. He calls me by the name which He announced to the heavenly angelic host the day I was created for His purpose.

Isaiah 43:1-3 - But now, this is what the Lord says—he who created you, Jacob, he who formed you, Israel: "Do not fear, for I have redeemed you; I have summoned you by name; you are mine. 2 When you pass through the waters, I will be with you; and when you pass through the rivers, they will not sweep over you. When you walk through the fire, you will not be burned; the flames will not set you ablaze.
3 For I am the Lord your God, the Holy One of Israel, your Savior; I give Egypt for your ransom, Cush and Seba in your stead.

I am NOT your girl, your trash, or a loser. I am not someone to be stepped on or stepped over. I am not your enemy, or a figment of your imagination. I am NOT a hopeless addict or a helpless drunk, a lost cause, or your pitiful excuse. I am not someone to feel sorry for. I AM a mother, a daughter, a sister, and a friend. I AM an author, a speaker, a leader, and a trusted servant of the Living God. I am a minister. I am a child of the King! I am a disciple, a friend of Jesus, and a warrior ready for battle!

Isaiah 49:1-3 - "Listen to me, you islands; hear this, you distant nations: Before I was born the Lord called me; from my mother's womb he has spoken my name. 2 He made my mouth like a sharpened sword, in the shadow of his hand he hid me; he made me into a polished arrow and concealed me in his quiver. 3 He said to me, "You are my servant, Israel, in whom I will display my splendor."

I heard a voice from heaven as my name was called, "And He who sits on the throne said, 'Behold, I am making all things new'. And He said, 'WRITE, for these words are faithful and true.'" (**Revelation 12:5**)

IT'S NOT WHAT I AM CALLED, BUT WHAT I ANSWER TO, AND MY NAME IS VICTORY!

About the Author

Julie Keene is the author of Coming Full Circle Blog at www.comingfullcircleblog.com which is currently taking readers through the Bible in a year. She is a redeemed addict who was saved by Christ from the streets that desperately tried to consume her.

Julie has helped pen the book, "Just Susan", with Susan Haynes Brogan which was published in January, 2016.

She currently continues to work for Jacob's Well Furniture and she regularly brings devotions to the women currently in the program at Jacob's Well Recovery Center for Women in Poplarville, MS.

Julie is a devoted Bible Study leader and volunteers doing media and sound at the church she attends.

For more information on how you can get involved with Jacob's Well, visit www.jacobswellrecoverycenter.com.

#JWGirl4Life
Jacob's Well Girl For Life

From Asa Haynes

Julie Keene writes with a purity and elegance I have seldom been able to find in anyone else.

Her life stories are inspiring reality checks about defeat and victory.

For all who read, these life changing experiences are the kind of brilliant and touching hope that makes you cry in a good way.

Julie's stories implore you to think deep, desire to break free and live passionately for something in every single moment of life.

The way she writes tells you that she passionately wants more out of every day!

~Asa Haynes~
Jacob's Well Ministries

Prayer

of

Salvation

"Father, I know that I have broken your laws and my sins have separated me from you. I am truly sorry, and now I want to turn away from my past sinful life toward you. Please forgive me, and help me avoid sinning again. I believe that your son, Jesus Christ died for my sins, was resurrected from the dead, is alive, and hears my prayer. I invite Jesus to become the Lord of my life, to rule and reign in my heart from this day forward. Please send your Holy Spirit to help me obey You, and to do Your will for the rest of my life. In Jesus' name I pray, Amen."

Psalm 40:2 - He lifted me out of the slimy pit, out of the mud and mire; he set my feet on a rock and gave me a firm place to stand.

29378710R00155

Made in the USA
Middletown, DE
17 February 2016